Why Customers Would Rather Have a Smartphone than a Car

Why Customers Would Rather Have a Smartphone than a Car

Relationship Retailing as an Opportunity

COR MOLENAAR
Rotterdam School of Management
and Director of Consulting Firm eXQuo

GOWER

Published by
Gower Publishing Limited
Wey Court East
Union Road
Farnham
Surrey, GU9 7PT
England

Gower Publishing Company
110 Cherry Street
Suite 3-1
Burlington, VT 05401-3818
USA

www.gowerpublishing.com

British Library Cataloguing in Publication Data
A catalogue record for this book is available from the British Library

ISBN: 9781472466563 (hbk)
ISBN: 9781472466570 (ebk – ePDF)
ISBN: 9781472466587 (ebk – ePUB)

Library of Congress Cataloging-in-Publication Data
Molenaar, Cor.
 Why customers would rather have a smartphone than a car : relationship retailing as an opportunity / by Cor Molenaar.
     pages cm
 Includes bibliographical references and index.
 ISBN 978-1-4724-6656-3 (hbk) -- ISBN 978-1-4724-6657-0 (ebook) -- ISBN 978-1-4724-6658-7 (epub) 1. Consumer behavior. 2. Electronic commerce. 3. Customer relations. I. Title.
 HF5415.32.M645 2015
 658.8'342--dc23
                                                                          2015005303

Printed in the United Kingdom by Henry Ling Limited, at the Dorset Press, Dorchester, DT1 1HD

Contents

List of Figures and Tables

Figures

Tables

About the Author

Professor Dr C.N.A. Molenaar is Professor of eMarketing & Distance Selling at RSM/Erasmus University Rotterdam (from 1999). Part of his assignment is the research into the behaviour and motives of customers. Another major part is the influence of the Internet and information technology and the impact of eCommerce. The consequences for physical retail and webshops are obvious. The research field is broad and includes psychological motives, communication triggers, the chances in society and the changes because of budget cutbacks. The fight on the High Street, different shopping hours, a reduction of margins and lack of loyalty are all results of the impact of the Internet on our private and business life. What is the future of town centres, local shops, brands and old fashioned communication?

Professor Molenaar is seen as one of the leading opinions on changes in business and the future of shops and webshops in the Netherlands. In addition to his own research he teaches eMarketing at RSM to undergraduates and postgraduates. All students are international students and the international aspect adds a broad scope of research. Partners of his chair are: Cap Gemini, Danone, GFK Retail & Technology, Microstrategy and the Dutch homeshopping association Thuiswinkel.org.

As founder and owner of the eXQuo consultancy he advises a variety of companies and organisations, including city councils. Master classes, workshops and presentations are given on a variety of topics based on his research, such as the future of shops, the future of town centres, the impact of technology and new business models. Assignments can be booked through CSA Celebrity Speakers.[1] Previous publications include *Shopping 3.0* (2010) and *The End of Shops* (2013).

Contact Details

Web: www.cormolenaar.nl   Email: cor@cormolenaar.nl
Twitter: disruptretail   University: cmolenaar@rsm.nl

---

1   See www.csaspeakers.com

Introduction

The speed with which technology is disrupting the established order sometimes takes your breath away. Today's markets change so quickly, not only because of digitisation or globalisation, but also because of hyper competition.

Daily Telegraph, *13 November 2014, Rita Clifton, BrandCap, p. B13.*

A few years ago there were no smartphones (introduced in late 2007 and by 2013 more than 1 billion had been sold) and no tablets (iPad in 2010). There was no digital television, but the Horizon from UPC (2012) made it possible to watch TV on any smartphone and tablet. Facebook launched in 2008, but only really became popular after it was floated on the stock market in 2012. In just a few years' time, these have become indispensable applications. These days we read about other innovations: driverless cars, drones, the Internet of things, interactive mirrors, Google glasses, smart watches, virtual reality, location-based services, iBeacons and of course Big Data for analyses. In the coming years, these innovations will become a part of our lives. The result will be still more changes, further innovations, even more varied apps and a disruption to many systems and processes.

The first signs are already on the horizon: Uber is an app for calling a taxi – young people no longer buy cars but only want transport (Uber makes this possible immediately). Software is no longer sold, but provided on a paid subscription basis (this is true of programmes for the PC such as Microsoft Office), while cloud computing ensures that we can consult our files from anywhere and WiFi enables us to be online everywhere we go. We quickly adapt to the new opportunities, and start paying for things using our smartphone (PayPal, Alipay, Apple Pay). We increasingly use Facebook on our smartphone and tablet rather than on the computer. We make online purchases with a tablet sitting on the sofa or even pay with our smartphones in the shops. We buy online at a webshop, wherever it may be located, from Amsterdam to the Silicon Valley or China. Borders simply don't matter any more.

A New World

A new world, a new customer and a new society are beginning to emerge. This has consequences for all the old structures and old certainties. Flexibility is in conflict with permanent employment contracts, shop opening hours are at odds with a demand for 24/7 shopping. A house with a garden in a suburb or village is in conflict with the number of single-family households that seek out the city because of a desire for the life style it affords (urbanisation). It is not only about accepting the new opportunities – we also adapt our behaviour, and even our budget, to these new realities. This disruption affects every facet of life and is initiated by all the new applications, but above all by the way we human beings adopt them.

We live differently, have different wishes and different preferences. *To deny these developments would be to deny the future.*

How is it, then, that there are still advisors and entrepreneurs who keep on saying that it will all work out? Who also deny these developments and customer behaviour while the evidence keeps on piling up: ever more empty shops, ever more irritation at old structures (such as parking costs), a steep growth in Internet sales and pressure on margins because customers know precisely what price is acceptable. These days you can hardly avoid bumping into the adverts in shopping streets: 30 per cent, 50 per cent, 70 per cent discounts are constantly being announced, and still there is no one in the shop. The signs can hardly be clearer, can they? Denying change and putting off taking action is simply asking for trouble. This is obvious when we consider the falling number of visitors to the High Street, while towns and real estate owners are reluctant to make any changes. Trying to forbid new developments and new (buying) patterns, and misunderstanding consumer behaviour, leads to increasing irritation and pushes customers even more to seek new alternatives, first and foremost in the Internet. The solution is to facilitate the new behaviour and new desires, as well as new purchasing behaviour – however painful it may be. It is a matter of building the future, our future.

Changes

The city centre will be transformed from a shopping precinct into a leisure time centre, with restaurants, cafés, cultural venues and fun (small) shops. Shopping centres have to inspire and motivate customers to come and buy, and cooperation between the shops has become essential for survival. The

Internet must be seen as an integral part of a hybrid concept, with physical shops that would be supported by the Internet and Internet behaviour in turn would be supported by physical shops: a single, integrated behaviour for buying, working and entertainment. We already devote between 7 and 9 per cent of our disposable income to Internet-related items such as smartphones, subscriptions, apps, digital television and online subscriptions. Since our income is no longer increasing, we save on food (shopping at Lidl instead of Tesco), clothing (Primark), household articles (Home Bargains) and of course we search the Internet for good deals. This way we make room in our budget for these new expenditures, which we consider indispensable. To respond to this demand we see a growing market segment of cheap providers. The top segment is doing well, thanks to the need to set oneself apart, while being 'stuck in the middle' is fatal. This is the playing field of the online providers, which are wiping out physical shops. The shopping landscape is changing fast. There are empty spaces at less desirable shopping areas, and shops are disappearing from villages. They will be fewer and fewer shops (around 30 per cent fewer), and those that survive will need to become increasingly fun places. It is a challenge to get customers to come in to the shop. New design, a different assortment of merchandise, surroundings that appeal more to the senses, ease of access, different opening hours and more service: all of these must be tried and tested to motivate the customer, but will it be enough? Don't we need to learn to live with disruption, with the new possibilities offered by technology, which change our lives? Is there still room for traditional shops with an outdated retail and logistics model? Is there a future for large shops in city centres that are difficult to reach, offer little parking and are subject to logistical problems when restocking?

But what is it that people want, anyway? Our behaviour is a clear indication of our standing in life and of what options we make. Knowing one's customer is essential, and the changes are very advantageous for customers, so that they will serve as a stimulus for still more changes. It is actually quite simple: customers want to be known and recognised. They are looking for their own dream environment, their own cocoon in which to shop, work and live. Customers want freedom of choice, not to have things imposed on them – otherwise they will become recalcitrant, and the result will be radical emotions.

Reluctance to Change

Life is increasingly complex: it is not only the Internet that has changed our lives, but a series of related developments – sociological and psychological –

in addition to technology, internationalisation and communication. All these aspects play a role in the disruption of systems and processes that we are witnessing. It is a question of either joining in and facilitating the process or else simply quitting. I find it frustrating that people keep talking only about *what* is happening, but not about *why*. It also frustrates me that developments and choices (such as buying online or the option of becoming self-employed) are neglected or dismissed. We keep on trying to maintain the old and see only the negative side of new developments. Why can't shops stay open on Saturday evenings until 7:30 pm, as is the case in many countries? Why are the shops open when there are no customers (mainly in the mornings and on Mondays)? And shopkeepers are surprised (?) if customers increasingly turn to the Internet to make their purchases. Why aren't some of the hedonistic aspects of shopping centres (light, sounds, colours, smells and shop design) used to make them more appealing to customers? Why isn't there close collaboration between restaurants and cafés? Why is there an ever greater offer (sales) but not demand (customer purchases)? Why is the supply (selling) always taken as the starting point rather than the customers (buying)? Why don't municipalities work on ensuring that the necessary changes are made in shopping precincts, and why are these areas and city centres not regarded as essential conditions for the life of a community? The *why* question regarding change is hard to answer, but a discussion on the basis of a preconceived standpoint is no discussion at all.

The Challenge

I regard the quest for the underpinnings of change as a challenge. I spent many months consulting scientific databases, reading books and speaking with experts both at home and abroad. I studied market developments in England and the US in particular, markets which are far ahead of the Netherlands. Along with the sponsors of my academic chair, we initiated and conducted research and spoke with the research teams. Cap Gemini, GFK Retail & Technology and Microstrategy turned out to have valuable sources and experts that could clarify and explain a wide range of developments. Discussions with Ward de Vin and Kees Jacobs (Cap Gemini), Patrick Langley (GFK), Corien van Rijn and Remco van Malten (Microstrategy) were inspiring and at times heated, but ultimately helped push open the envelope. I made two study trips with thuiswinkel.org to the US, including both San Francisco and Seattle. Visits to Apple, Google, eBay, Adobe, Amazon and Microsoft afforded increasing insight into the developments. The Shop.org Summit in Seattle provided an opportunity to speak with numerous retailers as well as providers such as Alibaba and Amazon. Contacts with Professor Kit Yarrow also proved enlightening, offering greater insight into the reactions of contemporary people. All in all, it was an inspiring voyage of discovery of the *'why'*. The scope of the research, from brain function to the design of city centres, from the Internet to shops, offered new insights. I am very grateful to everyone who contributed: the named sponsors, Marcel Roozeboom for his useful feedback, the students at Rotterdam School of Management /Erasmus University, and the companies and municipalities that commissioned the research. With this book I would like to pass on my knowledge and insights and contribute to a future that customers want.

A dream world where everyone is happy.

PART I
The World We Want

An ideal world that fulfils our individual wishes

A world of low costs and a wealth of services

A world where each of us is at the centre

Chapter 1

Look Now ... Buy Later[1]

During the holidays you enjoy spending your evenings ambling past the stands and shops in the picturesque spot where you are spending a week or two: somewhere in the mountains, by the sea or just in your locality. You are relaxed, free of stress since this is, after all, a holiday, and you are ready for something nice and cosy. Lamp-lit shopping streets and market stalls, the romantic illumination of a church, harbour or other 'must-see' attraction. You sniff around, rummage through all the stuff you never thought you would want to buy, and yet you buy it. What do you want it for? What will you do with it? It doesn't matter, you are happy with your purchase and when you get home you can always give it to someone as a gift.

After a delightful shopping spree, you look around for an outdoor café to have a drink or a bite to eat: Some local cuisine, of course, and maybe a refreshing drink. Life smiles upon you, and you are wonderfully relaxed. The shops and the cafés have clever ways of appealing to this happy tourist. Profit margins are ramped up by overcharging and through the game of haggling, though it must be said that we are not as good at it as the Chinese, for example. This kind of shopping is pure emotion, the Internet is far away, and the sense of satisfaction is here and now.

When we travel to distant lands, we have similar experiences. Shops in Asia or Africa are still of the old-fashioned type we heard about from our parents and grandparents; tiny little shops run by the owner or a real entrepreneur. They take an active approach to selling, and address customers directly if they can see from a mile away that they are tourists. *Where are you from? Holland? Van Persie, Robben – good team!* They will say anything just to be nice, for customers will buy things from nice people.

---

1 Extensive research into customer behaviour and preferences in the Netherlands was conducted by Cap Gemini (2014) as part of an international study titled Digital Shopper Relevancy Research 2014.

But shopkeepers are also happy to wait for their regular customers, people they know from their own street, neighbourhood or village. The shops make just enough profit to cover their owners' basic necessities. To succeed, the shopkeeper has to work long days, but that's just the way it is. Life unfolds on the street and in your shop: waiting for a customer is also a form of social cohesion with your neighbours, after all. A little chat, a game of cards or a board game, perhaps, a lot of time spent waiting and at the end of the day checking to see if enough money has come in to survive another day. The shops compete with each other for location, social cohesion, salesmanship and perhaps service as well. There is a large range of products on offer, often consisting of identical items, and the shops are in close proximity to each other, highly concentrated. Yet shopping is such fun for all the tourists. The shopkeepers know each other and are happy if business is good. Everyone wants to build up a little nest egg and social harmony between the various merchants is very important in those types of places.

Changes in Buying Behaviour

This kind of approach has in fact always been the rationale behind shops. The core values that determine the success of a shop were location, selection and entrepreneurship, along with customer loyalty. Shopping and getting one's groceries was something everyone had to do, but it could also be a social and sometimes even an inspiring activity. It's a nice way to spend some time with other people and chatting with neighbours. Thanks to growing prosperity in the past four decades, more and more shops have opened up, all with the same core values and the same structure. New shops appeared on shopping streets, which kept on getting longer. The shopping precincts expanded to include adjacent streets, making it possible for ever larger (core) shopping districts to emerge. Municipalities and project developers also fostered the establishment of new shopping precincts, based on calculations of capacity in a given place or region. Active branch policies (to manage the location of a variety of shops) led to the establishment of healthy city centres. The (local) government played more and more of a governing and regulating role and became ever more involved in planning policy, from issuing permits for shops and terraces in shopping streets to regulating opening hours. This increase in the activities of a municipality has been linked to ever higher burdens on shopkeepers and owners of commercial buildings. As long as people needed to go shopping, everything was fine, since customers were, after all 'captives' with no choice but to go to the shops. But now that this need is decreasing, with the rise of other options for making one's purchases, will the shopping precincts survive in their present form? Do we still need all those shops, and are shopping districts attractive enough for shoppers today to still want to visit them? At first, changes in buying behaviour emerge quite slowly. In addition to all the social changes, it was mainly the technological changes that influenced consumer behaviour.

First of all, customers have become increasingly mobile, so they can choose to go shopping in many other places. As a result, shopping centres have to be easily accessible. New shopping malls have been built close to motorways and fitted with large car parks so that customers can get to them easily. Next, we have seen the rise of commuters, and with them a clearer separation of home and work. In fact, people increasingly tend to go shopping near their places of work or on their way home. Shopping centres have been opened near office buildings or at other venues that attract large numbers of potential buyers: a football stadium with adjacent shops is one such example.

Initially, this development did not present any threat to existing shopping precincts, as there was economic growth; consumer spending was increasing and there was demand for more non-food shops, preferably with a touch of luxury.

These developments were all based on the same structure: a collection of shops, a balanced branch policy, rigid opening hours and a strict set of rules compiled by the local authorities listing what shops can and cannot do. To this day this is still the case, only the circumstances have changed considerably.

Can shops be open when customers want to shop, or do customers have to shop when the shops are allowed to open?

Over the last decade, it is the Internet that has made its greatest mark on buying behaviour. The Internet is a source of orientation and information, certainly, but is also a tool for buying directly, because all sorts of new devices such as tablets and mobile phones can access it. This has proved to be a catalyst for the changes in buying behaviour. Falling turnovers, pressure on profit margins and a critical, well-informed customer all present problems for the current retail sector. But the falling amount of disposable income has also led to a more price-conscious consumer, and thus discount shops have been doing well.

Impact of Internet Sales on Shops

Developments in the existing, physical shop structure and where new shops and new shopping centres will be built no longer depend solely on the economic basis of a location or region. It is a fact that consumers have flocked en masse to the Internet to do their shopping, and also increasingly use the web to find information. So, it is no longer the case that one has to go to a shop in order to make a purchase, but one *can* do so if one wishes. The Internet has become a threat to existing shops, shopping precincts and the solidity of the existing structure. Natural growth and shrinkage are part of the life of human beings and of organisations. And so a decrease in turnover and a fall in the need for shops and for shopping surface area is a natural process. But what about if this shrinkage is further accompanied by a less functional structure, which we can see, for example, among the less successful shops, with fewer customers and more vacancies? If the offer no longer matches demand, as is clear from the constant discounting of products in shops by up to 70 per cent? Can one then simply conclude that there is less need for shops or is there perhaps a need for different sorts of shops or a different shopping experience? Isn't the solution in such a situation to move from a supply-oriented policy to a customer-oriented one? To do so, one needs to understand customers' motivations when making a purchase, and to research the underlying causes of the new buying behaviour, the new approach to shopping.[2] Customers must once again be motivated to go to a shop and to buy at prices that still make a decent profit margin for merchants possible, otherwise there is no future for physical shops. Existing shops are under increasing pressure and customers are turning more and more to buying online. It is also true that nowadays the reasons for opting to make a purchase in a shop differ from those of the past. No longer is the decision driven by reason (I have to go to the shop), but it is emotion and inspiration that have become the most important reasons for shopping. Falling turnovers, lower margins and excessive stock are the best evidence of this.

WHAT IS THE BASIS FOR THESE CHANGES?

The changes in buying behaviour and in the retail sector have an underlying cause. Of course the Internet and technology are important factors, but that cannot be the only reason. Technology has to be applied and used. There have been enough technological developments that were never accepted and therefore failed. To determine the basis for the current changes, three factors are of prime importance:

---

2   See Molenaar (2010).

- *Human factors.* Why the Internet is now being used and people are prepared for change.

- *Technical technological factors.* Why are businesses using this technology in particular in order to stand out from the rest?

- *Socio-demographic factors.* Pressure on leisure time and other options for how to spend our free time. There are ever more single-person households and greater priority devoted to hobbies and social activities.

Underlying these three factors of change is the relationship between human activity and technology. What are the consequences of the reciprocal influence of human intelligence and the application of the technology (singularity)? Are our brains not being rewired by the Internet, giving rise to new forms of behaviour and different needs than, say, even five years ago? All these factors mean that it is not sufficient to simply defend the old ways of doing things, without considering the opportunities for change. This is as true for shops as it is for municipalities and interest groups.

Chapter 2

Human Factors as an Accelerator of Change

Most of the issues that face shops stem from their customers, who have alternative shopping choices. A number of factors are at play here, including demographic, psychographic and personal motives. All of these factors are influenced by developments in technology, such as computer capacity, accessibility of information and the development and use of novel devices.

Demographic factors include the age profile of the population of a given area, its composition, the presence of ethnic minority groups and the proportion of males to females. Young people shop differently to old people. Young people adopt new technologies quickly, whereas old people maintain a traditional approach to shopping. These two groups clearly demonstrate different behaviours, but said behaviours can also be the result of education, profession, marital status, living situation and gender. Insight into the structure of the population is key to mapping out shopping facilities, but the related group behaviours and motivations behind them are equally important indicators of change.

Psychographic factors are more concerned with personal circumstance and the distinguishing behaviour of one individual or one target group. Personal preferences, lifestyle choices and general behaviour fall under this category, but can only be measured if they are recorded by the customer in one way or another. This is where Facebook accounts represent a rich source of information, revealing one's preferences (Likes), behaviour and actions, which together help form an individual's psychographic profile. Not surprisingly, Facebook gathers a vast amount of information regarding purchasing preferences and predicted buying behaviour. Such external information regarding behaviour and interests can be combined with buyer information held by the webshop or retailer to paint an evolving image of the customer. When socio-demographic factors are added into this mix, it becomes possible to get a far better steer on buying patterns of a particular target audience. The customer, the individual, has quite literally become King as far as the direction in which shops today will develop is concerned. This signals the end of a supply-driven economy and the beginning of a demand-driven one – a shift, which leads to the structural changes, or disruptions, I will discuss later on.

Socio-demographic factors are what help create a profile of a particular target audience group. For individuals, psychographic factors and (buying) behaviour are what make profiling possible. These details are used as 'matching criteria' for the specified target group. If someone demonstrates the same socio-economic profile as the individual about whom we know everything, that person can be approached in a very precise manner. Be it via traditional media such as direct mail or email, or via direct messaging on their own websites or different websites. In the future, however, online and offline communication will be far more immediate and take place closer to the moment of purchase itself. Facebook and Facebook information is of tremendous value to the buying process and to customer recognition.

On the web, this exercise takes place in the form of behavioural analysis, but its practice is very sporadic in physical shops. The combination of (big) data and a mobile phone with location services enables physical behaviour to be led in the way described above. The battle towards mobile hegemony becomes a battle between Google and Facebook based on big data and client recognition.

Technological Factors

Technological factors revolve around a person's or a group's capacity to adopt new technology. This is largely reliant on the opportunities available to apply the new technology (structural reasons). With an increase in opportunity (i.e. growth in the number of apps and websites out there), people's acceptance of the Internet also increased. The uptake of the Internet could be clearly defined by age group, with the younger audience adopting the phenomenon first. But behavioural adjustments to accommodate new possibilities are also a considerable factor. Where previously there was talk of consumer pioneers, then 'early adopters', what counts nowadays is the 'first mover' principle: who accepts the new applications and who is prepared to modify their behaviour accordingly. This 'early adopters' group gives a good indication of what can and what will happen, hence the emphasis on young people's reactions to the launch of new applications or devices, such as a smartphone or smartwatch. This group is effectively a pilot group that determines the potential success – or failure – of a device. The fact that young people as a group are volatile and quick to change their views is only a good quality for a test group to have. Behaviour at this stage also demonstrates the amount of resistance there is. Other, often age-related groups, will take the lead from the youngsters, but trail somewhat behind. What emerges is a nice curve of the acceptance behaviour, but also the chance to stimulate demand and usage. Knowledge of the 'first mover' is of utmost importance to manipulate the 'slow movers'.

Technological factors also embody the ability to break through *structural constraints*. Structures are at play within society, our behaviours, within the spheres of home and at work, within the private sphere as well as in a trade environment. Structures provide security and guidance. They make it easy for us to predict what's going to happen and what's expected of us. The challenging of any structure almost inevitably leads to uncertainty and thus resistance. Examples from a private sphere would be a house move, divorce, the arrival of a new baby or redundancy. But the same principles apply in a commercial context, where most change takes place within a pre-existing structure. Resistance to change in a retail environment is based on this same uncertainty; developments are stalled because they act against the interests of a shop, shopping area or municipality. This attitude essentially smacks of disrespect towards the customer. To deny development and fail to react to customers' changing buying behaviour is only asking for trouble. Change creeps in eventually. But all too often, it's a case of too little too late.

Socio-demographic Factors

Socio-demographic factors relate to the composition of a target group: age, gender, marital status as well as factors such as income, profession and education. The target group's composition strongly dictates purchasing behaviour, Internet acceptance levels and expenditure. The primary Internet shoppers are young people and young families, in contrast to older people, who shop more selectively online and use the Internet as a resource tool. Education and profession are also important here, but have more of a bearing on general customer behaviour, choice of product and choice of shop. It is certainly not the case that the better-educated use the Internet more often, rather they use it in a different way. This information around customer behaviour is often accessible via external sources or analyses formed from objective buyer details. Socio-economic factors can either be obtained from profiles based on intake information, or from assessing buying behaviour.

The Challenge

New technology is first of all employed within an existing structure (for efficiency), in the hope that its introduction will help optimise that structure. Even the Internet was first introduced within an existing structure, bringing with it email (instead of post) and file transfers as quick, reliable and cheap alternatives to existing options. The concept of webshops followed, with new shops and multiple channels springing up out of nowhere. A webshop was regarded in much the same way as a traditional shop. It was only after other suppliers, who knew how to exploit the virtues of new media, came onto the scene that questions started arising around falling figures and other possible uses for the Internet were considered; uses such as the previously mentioned data- and analysis systems used by webshops. These reveal a wealth of knowledge on individual shoppers; knowledge which the retailers are not party to, even if they do have their own webshop. It is this gap in customer knowledge that represents a real hurdle for existing retailers to overcome in the face of webshops; if retailers aren't prepared for the new developments, they'll lag behind.

To illustrate the speed of technological development, Professor Andrew McAfee[1] takes the example of a game of chess. Imagine placing grains of rice on the squares of the board, starting with a single grain on the first square, then two on the next, double that on the next, then double that on the next square, and so on. By the time you reach the 32nd square, you'd need an entire year's rice harvest. By the time you reach the 64th square, you'd need more rice than has ever been produced. This is compared to Moore's Law, which states that computer capacity doubles every two years. According to his calculations, we are already as far as square 32 on our chessboard. Over the course of the next two years, we'll witness many new applications and a doubling of the computer capacity we know today! It would appear the near future has plenty in store.

Phases of Change

Change can be broken down into three phases:

> Phase 1: adapting existing systems and structures.

> Phase 2: applying new possibilities within the existing vision and context.

---

1   Brynjolfsson and McAfee (2014), p. 40.

Phase 3: complete renewal based on the new possibilities (disruption) and close integration of the digital and the physical.

The year 2014 was, as it happens, the year in which the realisation that the existing structure is ephemeral, hit home. Alternative solutions must be sought out. The immense pressure on profits and results are the reason why. Over the course of the last decade, the retail industry has optimised the trade structure (*Phase 1*). The route from manufacturer to consumer has been optimally structured through logistics, wholesale and shops. Supply functions and information functions are included throughout the process, which is underpinned by technology and based on supply. Whilst the information exchange between customer and manufacturer is slow, until recently it was effective. In fashion, for instance, orders were taken at the retailer, processed by the wholesaler/importer and passed on to the distributor/manufacturer. The latter placed orders with various producers of items, or bought in the necessary raw materials or supplies. After manufacture, the items retraced these steps, finally reaching the retailer after six months – or more – with payment due within six weeks, that is, prior to the sale. A successful entrepreneur had a good feel for their market, managing the balance between supply and demand. Cost-effectiveness was the overriding influence, leading to manufacture taking place somewhere far removed from the end consumer. Decision making took place on a low-cost principle, with a margin added at each transaction along the way. The market price was eventually determined on the back of this cost-plus strategy. At this first stage, new applications are mainly used to render existing processes more efficient. Efficiency is the sole driving force behind the first renewal phase. Investments in technology were assessed based on calculated return: the quicker an investment paid for itself, the better.

In the *second phase,* new applications are also grounded in an existing structure, but this time with a different purpose. The objective of cost-saving is replaced by quality enhancement, or increased efficiency as goals. Initiatives such as after-sales service call centres, (email) newsletters for direct communication and the launch of a webshop would all fall within the remit of the second phase. Often, the new application will make an old, less effective application obsolete. In the case of a webshop, this application sits alongside the existing shop. In essence, the webshop is another regular shop; the only difference being that it relies on a technological possibility (the Internet) … So far, nothing too revelatory.

Changes to structures seldom happen, given that this leads to uncertainty. Structures grant security and guidance and any deviation from their safety makes us feel insecure. The first phase of change generally leads to optimisation and greater efficiency. Only once this is exhausted, due to the status quo being placed under increasing stress, will discussions be initiated around possible changes to a structure. Those who approach things differently are mostly new, young businesses without historical baggage. When they are successful, the existing structure comes under even greater stress, at the expense of existing suppliers and market leaders. This is precisely what happens in retail. Altered customer buying behaviour, partly instigated by the possibilities of the Internet, puts pressure on turnover and margins of existing parties. Change is difficult due to existing (financial) constraints.

Disruption (Phase 3) always causes a stir, altering market conditions and changing market leaders and suppliers. Amazon is an example, as is Google, who challenged Microsoft, and Facebook, who in turn challenges Google, and recently Alibaba, who it has emerged is challenging Amazon.com. This interplay demonstrates the disruption of structures at work: from microcomputer to the Internet, from the Internet to mobile apps. These changes implore users to change and make use of the applications, which in turn adapt themselves to the altered behaviours of their users. The result is a decline in the use of the traditional medium – the shop – and therefore, change. This was most clearly illustrated when the introduction of the laptop computer brought computers into people's front rooms. And later again, thanks to the tablet and WiFi, when using a computer became possible anywhere and everywhere. The consequent effect on buying behaviour was enormous. Firstly, because the previous time restrictions on purchasing no longer existed, and secondly, because you no longer needed to sit behind a computer to buy: you could do it from the comfort of your sofa with a tablet in your lap. When computers used to be confined to the bedroom or study, Internet shopping was rational, with peak times between 7pm and 9pm. With laptops and tablets, online purchases are made on more emotional grounds, often in the living room in the company of others (and a glass of wine). The prime purchasing time has shifted to between 9pm and 11pm.

The book[2] *Leading Digital* also cites three phases to changing an organisation to better meet the demands of customers. These three phases are based on the transformation of the Burberry brand, which I will touch on later. Phase 1 states the need to acquire customer knowledge and instigate change from the outside in. More precisely, it states the importance of identifying what it is your customers want, and working out how you can modify your business (shop)

---

2   Westerman, Bonnet and McAfee (2014), p. 34.

to give them this. All too often businesses fall into the trap of thinking from the inside out and making adjustments that are not based on the knowledge of the customer buying process. An example would be rearranging the design of a store not to enhance the customer's experience in any way, but purely because the new layout is more convenient. Why should the till necessarily be by the door, for instance? Similarly, loyalty systems awarding customer discounts or points amounting to a free gift are conceived out of complacency, not because the customer derives any great benefit from them.

Phase 2 concerns customer communications: be sure to keep channels of communication open at all times, allowing you to reach customers 24/7 via social media, smartphone, apps or any other digital channel. This communication promotes connectedness and thus loyalty.

Phase 3 is to determine your strategy based on available data. Knowledge of the customer and of their behaviour should form the foundation of strategic decisions. It is highly disappointing that members of social media teams hardly ever get input into strategic decision making. These are the very people who have daily contact with the customer, yet they are not consulted. Perhaps it is because the management is ashamed of its very lack of knowledge that decisions are based on out-dated information and external advisors? This book ascribes a challenging future to leaders of this ilk.

DISRUPTION CHANGES EVERYTHING

Since the 1960s, the computer has exercised greater and greater influence on our lives, both in the personal and professional spheres. Its origins are in the processing of large data files and the optimisation of business and manufacturing processes. As a result, costs were saved, quality improved and mundane tasks could be taken over by machines, making work a whole lot more interesting. But this was merely the beginning of things to come. Automation meant automised actions were performed, which lead to consistent quality, greater prosperity and lower costs. The processes remained intact. Other innovations, such as the iron, the car and the telephone also grew on the back on existing structures, with a view to optimising them. In all, very little changed. But the changes that were to follow on from here were very gradual, virtually undetectable. Changes in information technology, in contrast, happen at a rapid pace, demanding an equally rapid response in order to keep up. In this sense, it is not surprising that existing companies have difficulty adapting to this change. All too often it is taken on board too far down the line, by which time the market and/or its customers have evolved further still.

Telecommunication companies struggled for a time with Skype and later, with WhatsApp. The impact of Skype appeared confined to the business model of telecommunication companies, as the 'caller' needed to be sitting behind a computer. This was indeed a barrier. Skype was only used for very specific applications, in scenarios where visual aspect was key, so for meetings, business negotiations or for chats with the grandparents in Spain. Mobile application of Skype remained a challenge. Telecoms companies adopted a wait-and-see approach to WhatsApp, even as its popularity rose. Interactive exchanges via mobile phone were having a detrimental affect on SMS traffic. Only once the business model, read revenues, began to suffer did the telecoms outfits start to react, by which point it was too late as the new, young WhatsApp had partnered with Facebook, which was turning its focus to the 'mobile' customer.

WhatsApp exemplifies disruption in the telecoms market. No longer are existing providers competing against one another. Instead, the threat comes from a new provider that's using the smartphone, Internet and WiFi in a whole new way: a new application for interactive messaging using the online possibilities of the Internet. Instant messaging versus slow SMS traffic reliant on traditional phone lines, and all its inherent limitations. But does the same not go for watching TV? Internet TV has become standard, with many channels offering supporting information. Nowadays it's not unusual to have two or even three screens live at once, enhancing viewer experience with additional and interactive information. Plain TV watching has almost become a thing of the past and certainly if you're watching something at the time of broadcast (national football games being the exception here). The when, how and where TV is watched is now at the complete discretion of the viewer and no longer dictated from the supplier's side. Watching TV on a smartphone during a train journey is no different to watching a live international football match at the pub. But what does this mean for the broadcaster's business model? Are adverts still effective, or are more sponsored programmes the answer? Perhaps we'll see a whole new business model emerge, one that's based on usage offers the option of adverts or no adverts, or perhaps something more creative still.

An old Japanese parable tells of a plant growing in a pond which doubles in size with each day that passes. After 30 days, the pond is completely overgrown. At what point do you intervene? Even by day 29, when the pond is overgrown by half, it's already too late to take action. This is precisely the dilemma existing companies are facing: premature intervention results in operational loss, while delayed intervention can mean the demise of the business. This parable is synonymous with the chessboard analogy used above. All of our greatest innovations have emerged over very recent years – from the mobile phone to the 3D printer. Over the coming two years, we can expect a doubling of current IT capacity: a breakthrough national WiFi network, a new, smaller and improved chip, and rapid analysis systems for big data, sensor technology and automatically driven cars. This will all be upon us within the space of a few years. New market players who make use of these new technologies have it easy, free from the burden of legacy systems and hot-under-the-collar shareholders or investors, but what about existing businesses? When should they jump on the bandwagon of change? Is it best to wait and see how the coming years unfold? Financial results and market developments within the retail sector suggest no alternative but to join in, now!

Businesses can be divided into four categories[3] based on the degree to which they are open to change and influence from digital applications. The first group are the 'inexperienced' companies; critical of change, often with a rigid hierarchy and whose sales are clearly supply-driven, often via a supply channel. Next are the 'conservative' organisations, which do utilise digital developments, but within structures already in place. They carefully weigh up the benefits versus the risks of change and base their decision on ROI (return on investment).

Wholesale change and a preparedness to execute changes quickly are characteristics of the next group, the so-called 'fashionistas'. These are modern businesses, hasty to adapt to changes in demand or market conditions. Fashionistas carry remnants of old structures, such as a hierarchical and/or departmental internal structure. Coordination between departments is limited, but digital applications are used throughout the entire organisation. Finally, there are the 'digital masters'. They enjoy a digitally focused structure, a hands-on leadership style and strong focus on customer benefit and added value. It is this very group that represents the disruptors: leaders of change and shapers of future structures. Amazon.com, Google, Apple and Alibaba are examples. The speed at which they operate and adapt is highly intimidating for existing businesses. This is evident in today's retail, but also in the banking sector.

---

3   Westerman, Bonnet, and McAfee (2014), pp. 15–26.

Chapter 3
Payment Traffic

Payments traffic is being taken over by new suppliers and it is becoming more and more commonplace for investments to be made via crowd sourcing and private investors. Failing these, take-overs and market flotation are always another option. The banks were simply too slow to keep up with the market developments and too late to start searching for second chances. Branch closures and staff reductions (which are likely to double over the coming years) are clear signals.

Speed of Action

The dilemma many businesses face is knowing *when* to act? Change is a painful process. In the short term, results will suffer and improve again only if the change made turns out to be a wise one. Andrew McAfee[1] notes that change driven by technology is nothing new. What is new is the speed at which change takes place. For all of the innovations the last century brought us, it can be said that the possibilities and impact they would bring with them were *underestimated* by the new generation (Y generation) and now the millenium generation. The young, new generation is behind new impulses. This is true of today, but equally true of times gone by. History repeats itself through the inability of previous generations to translate new ideas into new applications. Furthermore, older persons (aged 40 plus) do not realise that what to them appear to be small changes affecting specific areas, are in fact changes that will lead to a multitude of changes affecting a multitude of areas. Andrew McAfee argues that what's lacking is an ability to imagine, process and apply new ideas. Judgements are often made too soon and from an existing, familiar frame of reference.

Innovation is held back by our inability to process new ideas fast enough.

---

1   Brynjolfsson and McAfee (2014).

One should really approach all development and innovation from a neutral standpoint. Youngsters do this, as does a layman introduced to an unknown field. This is where we see the consequences of the transparency afforded us by the Internet: everyone has instant access to all kinds of information and can form their own opinions on whatever it is they come across. It is in the absence of knowledge and prejudice that fresh ideas come to light. The low start-up costs involved in realising an idea allow for tremendous creative regeneration on many levels. The Internet too is home to many niche providers and new and creative concepts based on the new Internet possibilities. Overnight success is no longer a far-off dream. Indeed, existing parties are prepared to offer large sums of money for ownership of the new idea. Unfortunately, just the opposite more often rings true: great ideas do not necessarily lead to great commercial success.

Out of the blue, a colleague comes along with a new and novel application. Innovations from the world of IT are driving other fields such as marketing, organisational studies and finance. All of a sudden, technology is calling the shots, and the reigning experts don't have the skills to handle it. *The greater the distance from the problem's core competency, the greater the chance of creative and successful change.*

Information within Everyone's Reach

There is something else at play here. The speed with which information travels is immeasurably higher than before, but access to the same information is unlimited. No longer is a small elite group privy to obtaining knowledge – now anyone can get hold of almost anything. A consequence of this is that people will form opinions on a whole raft of subject matters, often based on knowledge gained from some online research. *There are really no more excuses not to know something.*

Getting hold of information has become more important than being able to reproduce it. Just a decade ago, one applied learned knowledge at school or university. Knowledge was power. Decisions in the boardroom were taken based on hierarchy and amounted experience. The advisors who surrounded the board stood by its decisions, they didn't dispute them. Nowadays, the board has its hands full with mouthy management and employees who keep themselves informed (online) of current developments and who are able to very quickly locate information through the Internet. The tension is tangible.

So long as performance is good, there is no issue. But as soon as performance comes under stress, the cracks start to show.

This is precisely what became apparent in 2014. The cause of the issue is no longer the recession, but the altered buying behaviour of customers. Shops are offering too little added value. Why would anyone choose to pay a shop owner above the odds when his 'service' is of no benefit? Ordering directly from the manufacturer is a logical way to dodge the margins added on along the way. This disruption is in full swing, thanks in part to Alibaba. The added value shops are able to offer has shrunk due to the customer being in a position to seek out what they want over the Internet and then order it directly from the manufacturer. In this sense, shops have been robbed of their raison d'être, with vacancy as the consequence. Desperately trying to cling on to these shops is nothing but naïve. A far more productive approach is to re-establish what now constitutes added value for customers.

FORMS OF DISRUPTION IN RETAIL

Digital disruption in retail has the same characteristics as in other industry sectors. Aspects of change are: processes, data collection and analysis, communication, sales and products. Digitalisation has had an impact on buying behaviour, choice of location, shop and all other inherited physically determined factors. But what will change most is the focus, moving away from a supply-based product towards a customer-oriented service with a focus on customer requirements. This U-turn means that the future will no longer be about *selling* (motivated by sales) but instead about *buying* (motivated by customer requirements).

Digitalisation of processes, information, activities and even products leads to changes in supply and buying behaviour. An example of the digitalisation of processes is EDI (in the first instance), which facilitates the exchanging of data between businesses. Linking computers, systems and tills, for instance, made it possible to align business processes. This enabled the inventory function to be outsourced to an external party or the supplier. (VMI or vendor manages inventories is an example.) Supermarket stock is monitored in this way by the logistics provider or supplier. Advantages for the retailer are of course efficient stock management and reduced costs. A further development was the possibility of holding stock at an alternative location, for instance at so-called multi-hubs outside of the city. One manifestation of this development is the formation of 'city-hubs', providing local storage for all retailers in the city. With just limited stock held at the shop and an Internet connection, products are quickly despatched to the customer's home. In this manner, the shop becomes more of an experience or service point. Due to the minimal amount of stock shelved in the shop and smaller square footage, overheads are also reduced.

Data collection and analysis. Webshops possess a lot of customer knowledge and can target customers with pertinent information thanks to advanced analysis systems. The forerunner is Amazon.com, who claims to be able to predict sales one week in advance (70 per cent of the time). Not only is Amazon.com managing its stock better as a result, the company is also experimenting with sending the predicted stock to a local distribution point in advance to enable speedy delivery, sometimes within the hour. What matters most in digital transformation (disruption) is generating novel customer experiences, emotion and inspiration.[2] Shops cannot afford to stand by and watch latently. They too need to collect the relevant customer information and adapt their services accordingly.

Whilst banks look into the possible ways in which banking details can be used within current legislation, shops should be researching how they can gather relevant details. Perhaps via loyalty schemes, mobile data (sensor systems or iBeakons) or through home delivery. Such buying and buyer information must be collected and subsequently analysed on an individual basis. Shop sales need be continually analysed so as to be able to make immediate adjustments in response to customer behaviour. A webshop knows exactly what's going on in the 'shop' at any given moment. A retailer, on the other hand, only finds this out at the end of the week. Only then do discussions with the board begin. Already, the retailer is on the back foot. As well as structural changes, changes are also experienced in the various organisational functions. The Internet has influenced the retail sector at a communications, sales and information level, in addition to the infrastructure changes mentioned above.

Communication between the shop and customers or suppliers takes place far more efficiently through digital media. (Think of online invoicing, email and e-newsletters). Post is replaced by digital media and visits substituted for video conferencing. Yet despite these adjustments, there is but little evidence of disruption. A more accurate description here would be improved efficiencies to business operations. This is why decisions on whether to adopt computers and other forms of automation were initially based on revenue, cost-savings and cost recovery period. The form changes; the function doesn't. The use of information technology for the purposes of communication between providers

---

2   Westerman, Bonnet and McAfee (2014), p. 44.

and end users has led to radical change. Adverts have changed through their links to websites (think of banners) and the use of mobile phones or 'location based advertising' (at the time of sale). Google intensively analyses surfing behaviour of mobile users in order to better target customers with more customised ads. Traditional, physical methods of communication that were once disseminated via mass media have now become virtual and behaviour-led. Emails, e-newsletters, websites and affiliates (links to other sites) are just some of the changes that have been made possible. All of these new forms of communication revolve around digital application and personal interaction.

With regard to *sales function,* the physical site of sale was enhanced by a digital site of sale – a webshop (a digital interpretation of the traditional shop). But this is the same meat, different gravy. The real disruption began when suppliers started exploiting the virtues of digital media in conjunction with the webshop – portals, search engines, social media platforms and connectors. This depicts digitalisation of an existing methodology and an existing structure at its truest. This also brings with it a whole other set of skills and rules of play. You need to stand out, maintain relationships, lock-in customers and obtain a 'top of mind' position. This attitude is in stark contrast to the current situation within retail, where a quietly expectant attitude prevails. Retailers are not familiar with their customers and focus primarily on location and product range. However, getting customers through the door and convincing them to buy is a whole other matter.

Lastly, *products* are also digitalised, with a significant impact on existing structures. Products no longer need to be transported physically – they can be downloaded. This gives the Internet a huge head start over physical shops. Indeed, the first industries to fall victim to this disruption were those offering service products or non-physical products (such as data carriers). Travel agencies, the music industry, service industry, publishers and newspapers all suffered. When was the last time you booked a flight ticket with a travel agent and went into the branch to collect it? To add to this, more and more non-physical aspects of products are being introduced all the time. Think of after-sales service and customer care, upgrade and cloud services. These integrate digital and physical possibilities; a development that will only gain more ground with the introduction of mobile applications, WiFi and new devices such as 3D printing, Augmented reality and virtual cameras. Suppliers need more insight into the value customers ascribe to a certain product. Are these values purely physical, are they brand values, or does the value lie in the service?

Innovators offer more or less the same thing, but modify or accentuate certain aspects of their offering to suit the customer. Where for one customer the plus point might be speed of delivery, another might value made-to-measure customisation. These points of difference distinguish one supplier from the next. But they also make it possible to digitalise certain facets of a product more than others.[3] Price can be determined based on the value a customer attributes to the product, the service or outlet in question. If a customer sees added value in buying from a particular shop, they will be prepared to pay slightly more. On the flip side, where a customer perceives there to be no added value, their decision will be based on price point alone. In this scenario, the shop is at a disadvantage due to cost and risk levels. Such added value need not necessarily lie in the shop's product offering or their experience of that shop, it can come from other sources, too. The overall pulling power of the shopping precinct or area, catering options, accessibility and flagship stores all contribute to the perception of value. Buying behaviour at physical shopping sites is largely influenced by personal and hedonistic motives like emotion, inspiration, sensory stimuli and feeling.

Mercedes vehicles have special QR code stickers on their doors for rescue services. On scanning the code, the attendant is able to immediately locate the airbags, view the construction of the vehicle, the location of the petrol tank and other information vital to a rescue operation.

Developments in digitalisation will exercise huge influence on the retail sector, customer buying behaviour and the customer-supplier relationship. The question here may be can traditional retail still bring added value to these products? Judging by the fate of the publishing, music and travel industries, one could suggest not. Responding to disruption is difficult, but essential for survival. The latest wave of technologies, such as smartphones, big data analyses, social media and communication, serve only to break down the pre-digital paradigms of old.[4] Retaining these old paradigms equates to denying digital development.

Shops get modified, product offerings are tweaked, but the Internet also plays an integral part, with guidance using tablets, internet terminals and a direct link to the shop's own site.

---

3   Downes and Nunes (2014), pp. 6, 107.
4   Westerman, Bonnet and McAfee (2014), p. 54.

High street shops to get high-tech mannequins

House of Fraser in Aberdeen and Hawes & Curtis in London are among the first shops to start using beacon technology.

When a customer with an enabled smartphone app is within a 50m range of the beacon, they will receive an automatic alert about the content they can access. This includes details about the clothes and accessories displayed, such as price and links to purchase the items directly from the retailer's website, or where they can be found within the store.

The customer can also see more detailed photos and descriptions of the products, save 'looks' for later, share with friends and access additional offers and rewards.

Although beacon technology is already used in some public spaces such as museums and art galleries to convey information about historical artefacts, this is the first time that it has been designed specifically for a retail environment.[5]

The disruption within retail involves a structural change to the supply chain, the relationship between shops, agents, wholesalers and manufacturers. This change in structure is possible thanks to the application of Internet technology, but mainly down to the fact that customers wish to shop differently. The supply-led retail model, with its strong emphasis on transactions, gives way to a demand-led model with a strong focus on individual customer needs. This change evolves precisely as per the three phases described above. Existing suppliers are still preoccupied with Phase 1 (efficiency) and experimenting with Phase 2. The House of Fraser example illustrates Phase 2, in which the moment of purchase and the customer are central. Meanwhile, the likes of Amazon.com and Alibaba.com are in the full swing of Phase 3, with direct connections to suppliers, extensive analyses of individual customers (big data) and modifications to order logistics (such as Drones). Alibaba goes as far as to change the whole structure, the relationship between producer and final customer. The future of retail lies not just in close collaboration between the physical and the digital, but in an altogether new structure seated in the Internet's possibilities for connection. The current model is simply too costly and offers customers little added value. (This applies much less to daily grocery shopping than to shopping for non-daily items.)

---

5   *Daily Telegraph* (2014d).

Singularity: When Technology Dictates

Developments are happening fast. Existing suppliers find themselves under increased pressure and are eagerly on the look out for new possibilities. The application of digital technology is a must for success. As we have seen, the secret to this success lies in the integration of technological possibilities and personal knowledge and skills. And whilst technology plays a supporting role to human activity, a time will come (in the near future) when human actions are exceeded by technology. Computers automatically generate messages to customers based on sensor or recognition systems. Computers analyse information and initiate processes and actions. The automated messages reminding customers to re-order their favourite Nespresso pods based on calculated consumption are the first signs of this development.

Singularity is a loaded word with mathematical roots, taken to mean 'a value without limitations'. The term appears in both futurology and philosophy to predict future scenarios and to illustrate the possibility of computers becoming smarter than humans. Kurzweil[6] in particular established an interesting connection with Moore's Law, which states that computer capacity doubles every other year. His interpretation of the law is broader, as is Andrew McAfee's account of the law's impact. Kurzweil points out that Gordon Moore's law explored computer capacity based on transistors and integrated circuits, and that the prediction concerned the years 1965 to 2011, although many current-day predictions also presume constant doubling. He believes that the exponential growth in Moore's Law will continue beyond the use of transistors and integrated circuits to technologies which are yet unknown –inconceivable, even – to man today, and which will lead to technological singularity. Kurzweil describes this as 'technological change at such speed and to such degree, that it represents the breaking point for all existing structures and developments'.[7] This is interesting from a retail point of view for the application of the Internet and the ensuing effects. The sheer volume of knowledge which organisations can amass about their customers and their customers' buying behaviour on the back of extensive research into earlier mentioned psychographic and socio-economic aspects, coupled with purchasing aspects, means that these organisations will know more about the customer than he knows about himself. Amazon.com's claim, that it is able to predict 70 per cent of sales made in a week, is heading in this direction. Even

---

6   Chapter 1 of Kurzweil's (2005) book provides a particularly useful overview. See pp. 25–9.
7   An extensive description with illustrations is also available on Wikipedia. Available at: http://en.wikipedia.org/wiki/Technological_singularity

in isolation, this fact alone puts the competition on the back foot. During the next phase of development, this knowledge will be linked to existing functions and processes, giving birth to new developments that do not require human intervention, such as the case for communication, placing orders and product renewals. A link between a transponder, NFC chip and information database is enough for an automated order to be placed whenever a product runs out, or when consumption increases (printer toner, for example).

Technological singularity is a trans human[8] term with varying meanings. Many trans humanists believe that Moore's Law (which predicts a doubling in processor capacity within a specified timeframe) also applies to the speed in which science and technology develop. If this is the case, then the upward trend in technical development follows a wider exponential trend that must result in future singularity; to be precise, so-called *technological singularity*. In this state, technology governs everything that happens in society and organisations. The doubling in computer capacity Moore predicts will lead to this singularity. Even before this point is reached, large changes and adjustments to the possibilities of technology are already taking place. *Non-participation is impossible.* People get used to the possibilities and will come to demand them, too. This is already evident with the Internet, with people demanding shorter delivery terms, 24/7 shopping even at physical outlets, and demanding to be heard. Customers can't understand why shops should be more expensive when it is they who have to make the effort to go out and buy from them. The only route to survival is to go along with customer perceptions that are formed on webshops and Internet experiences.

---

8   This signals the arrival of the post-Darwin era where humans take evolution into their own hands.

Chapter 4
The Field of Futurology

In the field of futurology, technological singularity demarks the breaking point at which technological progression happens so quickly that humans with today's intelligence levels fail to understand the resulting society. Or, in marketing terms, when retailers are no longer able to understand their customers and are no longer able to react appropriately to change their offering. *It is naïve to think that the offer of free parking would be enough to entice customers back into town centres,* given that paid parking is viewed merely as a 'dissatisfier', or disadvantage. Paid parking thus carries a different value. If shops and shopping areas are less appealing, customers will make less effort to go shopping. Customers have less money to spare for travel and parking. Shops will only survive if they are able to motivate their customers. For shops, hedonic aspects (sensory stimuli, for example) are an essential point of difference in the face of webshops.

Technological singularity is generally understood to mean:

- *A point in the future when technological progression happens so quickly that humans with today's intelligence levels will fail to understand the resulting society.*

- *The point at which the first artificial intelligence or post-humans (improved humans with enhanced intelligence) take their own evolution into their own hands and begin to 'improve' themselves at such a rate that the world soon becomes unintelligible to contemporary man.*

Organisations need to make a decision around the implementation of the new technology. On the one hand, technology needs to meet the wants and expectations of its customers. On the other, it needs to be compatible with the organisation's processes and conditions. In his book, *Big Bang Distribution,* Larry Downes suggests a number of steps to take: talk to visionaries or experts who have a clear vision of the future and change; choose the right moment for market introduction. Start on a small scale to begin with, but don't spend too long testing. Take the example of the Amazon Kindle, which despite early teething problems, went on to adopt a dominant market position. Google's acquisition of YouTube and Facebook's acquisition of WhatsApp serve as further examples of quick take-overs based on vision and a belief in the future. Immediate market access and integration with existing services are of strong strategic advantage. The final point Downes mentions is cooperation with suppliers, customers and investor(s).[1]

Table 4.1   Classical approach versus disruptive approach

Traditional approach		Disruption approach
A focus on a single strategic disciple or overall strategy: low costs, best product or customer intimacy (Treacy and Wiersema)	strategy	Competition at all strategic dimensions at once. Good customer approach, cheaper and customised. Ensure constant innovation
Target a small group of early adopters first, then the rest of the market later	marketing	Approach all customer segments directly and secure capacity for quick upscale or exit
Look for innovation in cost benefits (low costs). Focus technology on dissatisfied or under-served customers	innovation	Start with low costs then experiment in the market itself. Combine components that can be used in various areas rather than developing new components over and over again

Source: Downes and Nunes (2014), p. 32.

Developments

Moore's Law suggests that technological progression is far from exhausted. Rather, it suggests that the speed of progression is actually increasing with the emergence of new applications. Singularity suggests that artificial intelligence will surpass human intelligence, leading to humans' inability to comprehend what's going on. Mankind will lose its ability to affect change. Technology will instead guide and steer change. Although this point has not yet been reached, predictions indicate that it isn't all that far off. It's a case of just a few decades, in fact.

Large corporations struggle with this change. It isn't by coincidence that big retail chains are also finding it a challenge, be they Marks & Spencer, Macys or Wallmart in the UK and the US respectively. Radioshack in the US,

---

1   Downes and Nunes (2014), pp. 111, 124.

for example, is going under at the mercy of the Internet. The once leading technology retailer with hundreds of small shops is being forced to give in to niche online players and professional retailers such as Amazon.com. Existing organisations draw on past experience and existing resources. The resources are often also owned by them – from computers to software to shops. These organisations are not (yet) adapting to the changes taking place by utilising new tools, or commonly accessible tools such as cloud computing, sensor systems or mobile applications that go beyond the scope of an app.[2] Businesses need to work together in the closest way possible in order for renewal to take place. This is true for manufacturers, brands and retailers, but customers should also be involved. McQuivey clearly states that only partnerships that share each other's risks and successes will come up with new ideas and thrive. Besides a will to work together and change, what this calls for is a digital mind-set. A digital platform on which product efficiency and customer satisfaction can be measured: a continual process of analysis of customer behaviour, customer satisfaction and product criteria. Consequences must be linked to this. Coolblue does this by putting customer satisfaction at the forefront with an NPS score, continuously monitoring this customer satisfaction and striving for better results. At the product level, product managers are responsible for customers and products, with videos supporting buying behaviour. The integration of supply and demand requires a self-made digital platform. Customer satisfaction and customer interaction are integral to this, but also represent a rich resource for marketing and marketing communications. The mistake that many organisations make is incremental innovation: introducing small changes, bit by bit. These small innovations are based on existing processes, methodologies, products and visions and do not lead to great success.

A woman can be a little bit pregnant no more than to innovate you can be a little bit innovative.

It is very important to think of renewal and possibilities with an open mind. A 'green field' or 'blue ocean' approach is the basis for an ideal strategy for innovation.

Emotion or Reason?

Shopping is about inspiration, experience, atmosphere and entourage, it is a brief escape from everyday reality and a chance for you to create your own

---

2   McQuivey (2013).

dream world with the help of the retailers. This is a form of pleasure, hedonism and enjoyment. The literature on this topic accurately distinguishes between emotional and rational shopping. Previously, this distinction was less relevant as people *had* to go to shops. The chief competition came only from the weekly market. Nowadays there are many more choices and factors that interfere with buying behaviour, including the role of the Internet, use of mobile devices and the power of social media. In addition, limited disposable income, free time and other socio-economic factors, such as single-family households, also play a role.

There are also differences in behaviour to be noted when purchasing daily items versus non-daily items. The role of the Internet is different for food and non-food items. I will expand later on these aspects in relation to customer buying behaviour and the influence of new media such as the Internet. The basis for change is the new customer buying behaviour. If this is not embraced, if all that happens is that existing structures are optimised, if change is blocked (by municipalities, governments or interest groups), then customers will make other choices. They will shop online, at other locations or at other outlets. *Preventing change is denying yourself a future.*

BUYING LATER, BUYING DIFFERENTLY!

Whenever we needed to buy anything, we'd go to the local shop or jump in the car and drive to the closest village or precinct. We still do this now, but less frequently thanks to the growth of Internet sales. Currently, we purchase 20 per cent of non-daily items, 2 per cent of food and 50 per cent of service products (digital products) online.

This growth is expected to continue in this way for the time being. All things considered, we can safely conclude that the Internet plays an important role in modern day customer behaviour. Analyses of sales streams show that with the growth in Internet sales, economic support for local shopping centres and town centres comes under strain. Similar growth in Internet sales is expected over the coming years, with perhaps even greater growth than expected with the arrival of Amazon and perhaps other foreign providers. Dutch webshops, Bol.com for starters, will certainly benefit from this competition. What is it that makes the Internet so appealing and why would customers still visit physical shops if no longer necessary? This is a real problem, not only for shops, but also for owners of shopping centres and municipalities. *People are buying differently these days. What chance is there still for physical shops?*

SHOPPING MOTIVES

The initial question concerns the appeal of online shopping and the advantages/ disadvantages of physical shopping in the eyes of the consumer. Secondly, we might ask: what next? The previous chapter discussed the impact of the Internet on retail, illustrated in three phases: efficiency of existing methodologies, efficiency within existing structures and lastly, change through the integration of digital solutions with physical applications. The merging of the physical with the digital – the hybrid concept – is a recent development making it possible to buy online, in the shop. Parallel to this there is a shift in focus, from supply-led (transaction based) to customer-led (needs based). These changes mainly affect suppliers, manufacturers, retailers and service providers. Of course what matters ultimately is consumer buying behaviour and the effective deployment of new technology. Based on customer behaviour, we can identify two types of purchase: emotional and rational. That is, hedonic (emotion and feeling) and utilitarian (goal-oriented). This distinction has a bearing on buying behaviour, but also on the application of new media during shopping and on the role of the Internet. Shops win on emotional grounds, whereas the Internet wins on

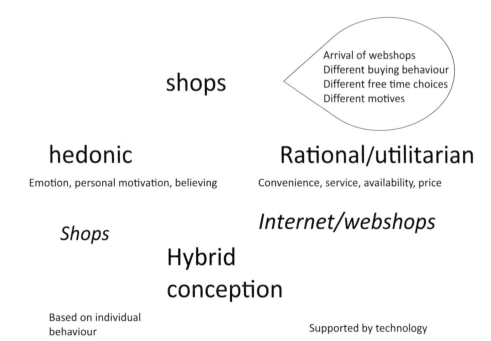

Figure 4.1   **Difference in shopping behaviour and motives between store and the Internet**

rational grounds. Thanks to new technological possibilities, what emerges is interaction within individual buying behaviour during the customer journey (the purchasing process). This is known as the hybrid concept.

Hedonic/Emotional Shopping

Personal considerations come into play precisely when there is a choice to be made as to *where* to buy. Going to a shop has become a choice: the Internet and other shopping centres are always alternatives. There are six emotional reasons why people go to shops:[3]

1.   For a feeling of *adventure and excitement*, and sometimes to escape 'reality' and enter a dream world. Adrenaline levels rise and you reach a sort of 'high'. This often happens when you unexpectedly come across sales reductions or offers, a new shop or a new collection. If price perception is low in these instances, shoppers get the feeling of 'too good to miss', or they get greedy.

2.   *Social reasons*, to shop with company or meet others. Men go together with other men to view cars or check out electronics superstores. Women meet up with other women for a spot of (recreational) shopping, usually for clothes. A cup of coffee on a terrace adds another dimension to the shopping.

3.   *Reward*, particularly if you're feeling low or you have achieved something good. Shopping reduces feelings of stress and promotes a sense of well-being. A purchase only adds to this feeling. You might buy yourself something nice, a little treat.

4.   *For inspiration*, to look at the latest trends, fashion or the latest technology. (The last example applies mainly to men who browse electronics superstores). It may be a visit to a designer shop or to Zara. Or a nosey through shops selling trinkets and vintage items. Homeware stores and shops selling regional produce are included here, as are boutiques selling their own collections. These are exactly the sorts of shops that fit within the new city model described in this book (emotion).

---

3   Arnold and Reynolds (2003).

5.   *Servitude*, for example buying for others, running errands or gathering information on what to buy and what not to buy to pass on to others. Older persons with enough spare time enjoy looking around for nice things to buy their children or grandchildren. Neighbours look or buy on behalf of each other. Feeling useful and helpful brings another dimension and a special feeling.

6.   *Bargain hunting*, looking for good deals or something really unusual. The old hunter instinct re-emerges here: *Men are hunters, women gatherers.* The first is all about the lowest price, the second about a reasonable price for a nice product. You feel like your shop has been productive.

The above reasons can be summed up in three main motives:[4] pleasure, arousal and escapism. The reason for shopping can thus be very personal. But it is led by how you feel. It might make you happier, provide excitement and arousal or provide a temporary escape from reality. It's all a question of feeling, and this is what constitutes the main difference to rational shopping whereby shopping is a necessity, not a choice. If shops and shopping areas want to attract and motivate customers, they need to cultivate pleasure, excitement and a certain feeling. As far as grocery shopping is concerned, this is rational, out of pure necessity.

Shopping areas, shopping centres and city centres will only be successful if they meet these criteria. There is a clear relationship between the attractiveness of a shopping area and spend on shopping. We see the same correlation between daytime catering facilities and the number of shops in a shopping area; one helps drive business to the other. And so the more pleasant and attractive somewhere is as a place to shop, the higher the consumer spend and the better the takings.[5] This also partly explains the issues shopping centres are confronted with today. Recent years have seen too little investment in town centres (in particular) to keep them pleasant and attractive. What's more, customers have had the option of visiting nicer shopping centres or surfing the net, making the situation increasingly challenging for retailers, if not impossible. More vacant properties only added to the negative perception of towns, creating a vicious circle. Unless this circle is broken, existing shopping centres will lose out to new shopping centres or outlet malls, which provide an all round more enjoyable experience.

---

4   Monsuwé, Dellaert and de Ruyter (2004).
5   Collum (2013).

Webshops, meanwhile, are getting better and better at identifying customers' needs. The use of new technologies (3D technology, smartphones, videos and sensor systems to name but a few) and data analysis to learn more about the customer make it possible to adapt far better to customer behaviour and purchase opportunities.

In logistics terms too, webshops are beginning to resemble physical shops more closely. Delivery of orders is fast and scheduled for specific times. Future Internet developments clearly lean towards hybrid concepts, an integration of the physical and the virtual (such as augmented reality, which combines real-life images with other images), location-based services and location-based communication. Customers are assisted by the possibilities of the Internet when shopping at physical shops, which will put further strain on the future town centres. Increasingly it boils down to experience and other 'hedonic' aspects of physical shops and the shopping environment. Matthew Collum concludes that retail managers must begin to appreciate the importance of the shopping environment as a whole. That is, the environment surrounding the shop, including entourage, opening hours, accessibility, variety of shops, catering and entertainment. Municipalities and owners of shopping centres have a huge responsibility here. That is, if they attach any importance at all to maintaining a pleasant town centre and nice shopping area. To stick to the old structure and belief that all shopping should be done in the town centre is naïve. Shopping streets would benefit from becoming more of a hedonic platform for customers, offering quality food outlets and artisan shops selling local delicacies. Why must every town centre consist of the same old chains? What is the appeal to new customers? Far better to research the customers' needs, review purchasing processes and stimulate desired behaviours or adapt the current offering to meet new patterns of buying behaviour. Change can be a painful process, but non-change will only result in more vacant shops and even fewer visitors to town centres and shopping centres.

Rational Shopping

Shopping on the back of emotional motives is only one way of shopping. Rational shopping (practical shopping) is another way. The primary concerns here are necessity and ease. Practical considerations such as location (close to home), accessibility (by bike or bus) and the availability of products are important. The conditions here are different to those described for hedonic shopping and rational shopping is often regarded as grocery shopping.

Different buying motives apply for (food) supermarket shopping than for non-food shopping. It is rational shopping that takes place locally and is shaped by convenience, availability, habit and routine. Rational purchases occur most often within food, but can also happen in non-food. It depends on the emotion the customer has invested in the product, as well as routine and necessity. Product availability at local shops is a good reason to buy. We will come back to this point later.

Since the rise in popularity or adoption of Internet shopping, an alternative to physical shops has arisen. Webshops possess more knowledge of buying behaviour and motives than physical shops, allowing them to better communicate with customers. In addition, developments in technology have meant that customers are far better supported during their online shop through the likes of product suggestions, customer interaction, instant customer support and video support.

When choosing between online and offline shopping, (travel) time and cost play an important role.[6] Offline shopping is often combined with other cultural or leisure-time activities, and includes shopping during a lunch break or on the way home from work. Where such activities are combined, the travel time and cost no longer matter. This means that offline shopping should no longer be seen as an independent activity, in which case the barriers of time and cost are too high. Shopping areas have to offer more than just shops, especially ones that do not look sufficiently attractive to bring in customers. A mix of cultural attractions and food outlets is a good solution for a shopping centre. In the case of outlet malls, it is precisely the integration of experience, fun, food outlets and small boutiques that is appealing. Choices have to be made as to how to attract and retain customers with more than just shops alone. In the United States, shopping malls are increasingly being placed near retirement homes. A visit to a relative in the home can be combined with a trip to the 'mall', and vice versa. Both have a shared need for accessibility and parking space so can be nicely combined.

Ludin and Veira's (2013a) research also indicated that women have a more negative attitude to online shopping than men. Recent developments, however, have meant that women are also increasingly connected to the Internet through chat functions and social media such as Pinterest and Facebook. Nevertheless, differences in online and offline shopping behaviour between the sexes remain. Since women spend more money during physical shopping, this is also an

---

6   Ludin and Veira (2013b).

interesting group for online merchants. The wider array of products on offer, the lower prices, quicker delivery and more secure payment methods are important (rational) elements that make webshops interesting to women as well. Discounts are also extremely effective, creating the impression that there is an advantage to shopping online. The most important factor, however, is trust: trust in the webshop and trust in the payment system.

Webshops now also appeal to women on more emotional grounds than in the past: forums, chat rooms, customer reviews and videos play an important part in this regard. Research conducted by Bassam Hasan shows that 'high touch' items are the ones that are most often sold offline and 'low touch' items online. The difference between the two is very personal and depends on the time available and on what can be found locally. If you have enough time, shopping is fun but not very efficient. If you have little time, online shopping is efficient, but a little less fun. It has a lot to do with the way people want to spend their free time.

> In 2014, Easter Saturday was a beautiful day on a long weekend. The perfect shopping day, in other words. Yet in-store sales were down considerably and online shopping had risen significantly. The combination of beautiful weather and free time inspired people to 'go out', indeed, but to the beach and amusement parks. A lot of time was devoted to hobbies and eating outdoors. The Internet was the 'escape' from shopping.[7]

A hybrid approach can bridge the distance between high touch in the shop and direct online ordering via a terminal or mobile phone. The challenge for the retailer is naturally ensuring that customers shop in your store rather than order from a competitor or from a brand direct. Through judicious use of WiFi connections (in combination with iBeacons) and terminals, retailers can target behaviour appropriately.

Men versus Women

Men and women behave differently when it comes to shopping. This is true both online and offline. Men spend more time shopping online and buy much more via the Internet than do women.[8] Although the differences are

---

7   Ludin and Veira (2013a).
8   Hassan (2010), pp. 597–601.

narrowing these days since women have begun to accept this medium, there is still a difference in women's perception of online buying (less positive). The study cited above suggests uncertainty as the main reason for this. Payment options, consumer care and product quality are the downsides: will anything go wrong, and will the items be what I expected? The research by Hasan also indicates that women tend to buy more on the basis of emotion, and men on the basis of reason. There are often notable differences per product group. Men buy according to feeling when it comes to electronics and hobby supplies, while women tend to buy those sorts of things based on reason. Men will compare the different technical features based on content (a computer's processing speed, the size of its hard drive) while women make the decision more on the basis of ratio: a computer has to work and must suit me! Women find the emotional and psychological experience of (physical) shopping important. Offline shopping has the advantage of personal contacts and social factors, while online shopping is associated with convenience, price advantage and efficiency. Developments in recent years, in which the Internet has increasingly come to serve as a social (social media) and communication platform (mobile phone), account to a large extent for why women are slowly leaning towards using the Internet on a smartphone. The trends in shops, where savings are made more and more through cheaper staff, reduced product assortment and less spending on the fun aspects of the store design, linked with the chaos of repeated price discounts, have not had a positive effect on shopping. The hedonic, emotional value of shopping has fallen because shops looked only at costs and not at the motives for buying.

Table 4.2   Difference in shopping behaviour

Offline shopping	Online shopping
Social, emotional, hedonic	Rational, functional, individual
Part of a number of activities involving fun and friendship, coffee shops	Part of a conscious customer journey, purchasing process. Emotion is led by video and social media
Feeling, seeing and buying	Looking, considering, buying, deciding (after receiving the items)
Difference between doing the shop (quick) and shopping (fun)	Difference between repeat purchases (preferred website) or first purchase via search engine or on recommendation
Travel time and cost are annoying	Waiting for delivery is annoying
Buying local	Buying anywhere, including from abroad

Tip-offs and Word of Mouth

In recent years, online shopping has been increasing. Growth in Internet sales is due to a lesser extent to new users, but more often to existing customers who buy more and shop more often. This is a clear sign that confidence in online shopping has grown. No doubt this is due to positive experiences with previous online purchases, reassuring customers that their expectations of what they are buying are in line with the reality of what they get. Others' experiences and recommendations are playing an increasing role. Everyone has some advice or opinion to give, and that includes you. We receive many tips from friends in the course of ordinary conversation, but posts on social media may also lead us to specific websites. Confidence in the advice given will depend on your confidence in the person offering it as well as on your own experience. The appeal of online shopping previously lay in its convenience factor, but the information and knowledge the Internet offers are another factor with increasing appeal (*cognitive*). In addition, there is a greater emphasis on social and emotional experiences (*affection*). As a consequence, online shopping can be divided into two types: goal-oriented (cognitive) based on knowledge, information or experiences, and fun-oriented, supported by mobile media that make it possible to surf any time and anywhere, often using free WiFi.

Websites take advantage of this development by making it possible to find products quickly via a search engine, and by offering products directly to customers based on historical buying behaviour. But also by incorporating effective elements in the web design, by means of consistency, interaction and fun. Examples of these are the site layout, photos, videos and customer interaction (reviews). Bassam Hassan similarly concludes that technological developments have reduced the differences in (buying) behaviour between men and women when it comes to online and offline shopping. Apps, mobile phones, beacons and similar innovations will considerably increase the acceptance of technology and its application in daily life and in shops, thus leading the researcher to further conclude that the online consumer is the consumer of the future. What we are looking at is no longer a dual or multichannel retail approach, but a hybrid consumer.

The Hybrid Consumer

A hybrid consumer is equally happy to shop online or offline, and will also buy via the Internet from the offline shop, or may consult the Internet while shopping. Hybrid consumers are guided by their own preferences and motives, and use each channel in the way that best suits them. Thus they may take a look first online, then go to the shop to have a look at the product in the flesh (showrooming), only to then go back and make the purchase online – sometimes whilst still in the physical shop. It is also possible, of course, that while shopping you will come across items that you never planned to buy, but that you look at online anyway in order to compare information or prices. This new shopping behaviour is stimulated by mobile applications. In addition, people in recent years have become much more technologically savvy thanks to the many developments in this area, and are able to combine different activities without effort.

> *Acceptance often develops in three stages: Adoption - you accept the new application and look to see if it can be of any use. Adaptation - the new application is the basis for a change in behaviour and, finally, Integration - whereby the new application becomes an integral part of overall behaviour. At the moment, the Internet is fully accepted and everyone uses a particular application (adoption). New developments give rise to new applications, making the Internet the basis for certain types of activities, such as watching TV and phoning via the Internet. Ultimately, the physical and virtual will merge into each other.*[9]

This is more applicable, of course, to younger rather than to older people, but that difference is rapidly disappearing. Despite the typical physical elements of offline shopping, the Internet is becoming increasingly important both at shopping centres and in shops. The number of traditional consumers who buy in local shops and deliberately go to the city centre to buy things will continue to decrease.

The developments in the market suggest a dichotomy between rational shopping, with price being important, and emotional buying, where loyalty and feelings are what count. In the first group, price is assumed to be the key element. This can apply to repeat purchases of essential items or merchandise with low emotional investment. The purchases may be made via the Internet, since price transparency is one of the great advantages of online purchasing, but they may also occur in physical shops. Supermarkets are under pressure from the low-cost shops, a sector in which Aldi and Lidl are the major players. Customers no longer want to pay over the odds for comparable products and attach less and less importance to service and to the shop's surroundings.

---

9   Hassan (2010).

This phenomenon is leading to a shift in consumer buying behaviour towards these merchants. Many countries are seeing the emergence of shops similar to Lidl and Iceland in the UK, which sell at very low prices. Technology has made it easier to transport frozen foods with longer shelf lives and this is why Iceland, with its low running costs, can keep its prices comparatively low. Bulk packaging also creates greater efficiency (and hence lower costs). In the non-food sector also, more and more retailers are adopting a no-frills concept, but still providing their customers with an element of novelty. These retailers often sell bulk goods and end-of-line items. A very efficient supply chain, shops at low-cost locations, a no-frills shop design and low purchasing costs combined with large volumes mean low prices. Increasingly, consumers are refusing to pay higher prices and are buying from these shops. There has been a considerable buzz around these stores, making them trendy and able to attract a large target audience. Support from the Internet is not applicable – at most, there is a basic website with the store addresses, which costs next to nothing to produce. On the Internet we see a growing number of suppliers of cheap products, mainly from abroad. Amazon.com goes by the strategy of 'cheapest'. Its principal aim is to ensure that customers can always get things cheapest from Amazon.com, and prices are adjusted several times a day as soon as it transpires that someone else is offering it cheaper. Chinese retailers are also enjoying increasing Internet presence. Following the initial public offering of Alibaba – China's largest webshop – entering the Western European market has become a greater priority. Quick delivery, 24/7 service and payment security with Paypal, among others, can facilitate rapid acceptance of Alibaba and associated webshops such as AliExpress. This will make online competition in the low-price segment even fiercer. Physical shops will soon be able to compete on value-for-money only, including shops in the low-price bracket.

Vocal consumers who keep themselves fully informed appear to be a desirable target group. A no-nonsense approach in low-cost shops is a growing phenomenon. Discount suppliers, especially from abroad, also see this target group as desirable. The result is a clear division of retail into three segments: *a low-price segment* with a no-frills approach, fiercely competitive on price, with location playing an important role. Generally, a cheap location is sought out and an optimal product offering is made possible through very efficient logistics. Primark and similar low-cost merchants combine safeguarding their brand image with a well thought-out PR policy and a strong focus on their target group (women under 35 with a limited budget). Primark has built a popular image at A1 locations, making it a magnet for the entire shopping area. This has made the chain stand out as it serves to draw the target group (young women with a modest budget) to the shopping street where it is located.

Second, there is a *top segment* for the most extensive budgets, with well-known brands that clearly play on emotions, associations and identification to make the buyer feel special. Buying the products becomes a special experience in itself. In specialty shops, often flagship stores, the image of the brand is strongly promoted and buyers feel as though they are a part of a dream world for the select few. It is this physical and emotional experience that is important, along with a sense of loyalty and identification with a clear target group. Every possible hedonic element is harnessed to entice customers. Shopping is a celebration that goes hand-in-hand with optimal service. Following the purchase, wearing the item confers self-confidence. After all, we all enjoy being complimented on a dress, bag, watch or suit.

Finally, there is a *middle segment* with few distinguishing features, a grey area in which the Internet in particular is gaining ground. This is in fact the most problematic segment within the physical retail sector. Customers get turned off such shops because they have nothing distinctive to offer, and for the most part, no specific focus. Often these are the shops that once enjoyed an A1 location. But in light of the new buying behaviour, where buying from a shop at all has become a choice, these types of stores are under threat. This group *has* to make changes in order to attract customers, win their loyalty and motivate them to buy. If not, they may well have reached the end of their life cycle.

The Primark Effect

Primark produces fashion for modest budgets and specifically for girls/women between the ages of 16 and 34. Primark generated a lot of hype thanks to its low prices, 'finite collection' and 'fast fashion' – also referred to as 'disposable fashion'. Reorders are impossible, and by means of a well thought-out marketing policy. This goes hand in hand with a self-imposed limit on the number of stores (a maximum of 30 in the Netherlands, where there are currently eight (2014), with two more opening in the autumn). This creates scarcity, while demand for items is high among the target group, partly because of Primark's low pricing. Primark is an excellent example of 'disposable fashion', since the merchandise is fashionable and very affordable, but will only be worn for a short time. You don't need to wear the clothes for very long and you can respond very quickly to new trends, at a low cost. Thus chains like Primark come up with fashion trends in rapid succession to ensure that customers keep on buying. Clothes of a previous style are quickly discarded as 'out-dated'. In addition, Primark has a well thought-out PR policy that puts it in the news time and again. A conscious decision was made not to open a webshop, which would detract from the sense of scarcity and thereby affect the number of shoppers who visit the shops. But cost also plays an important part. Running a webshop is expensive, as are logistics. This makes it difficult to keep the costs and prices as low on the Internet as in the physical shops. However, in 2012 Primark did sell some merchandise via Asos.com. The trial ended at the close of 2013, in spite of the fact that the sales were a success. Primark's focus is principally on the physical shop, the associated emotion and therefore the impulse purchase, and even more importantly on optimal cost control. It is precisely the creation of a sort of dream world, with surprises in the collection (rapid turnaround), trendy selection and very low prices that stimulate impulse purchases. This is the power of a store, and the same effect is not really achievable on the Internet. The website was too expensive and the partnership too costly, since the profit margins had to be shared.

> The boss of Primark's parent company has hinted that a trial to sell its clothes through online fashion retailer Asos is unlikely to continue. George Weston, chief executive of Associated British Foods, said: 'The trial has ended and we are exploring our options, but as you can imagine, the margins are so small that it can be difficult to sell a £3 t-shirt when you're spending the same amount just to ship it. The shipping cost for an online business is the key reason why online-only retailers can't compete with us.'

> He added that there are no plans for Primark to launch its own online business, suggesting customers prefer coming to stores.

> The growth of Primark was mainly due to its European expansion with 19 stores opened this year and a further 20 planned for 2014. Sales were up 5 per cent on a like-for-like basis.[10]

The Primark concept is still very successful. But in the older markets (Ireland and the UK), Primark has become a normal retailer with a recognised and specific type of product suited to its target group. In these countries, Primark is a regular feature of shopping centres, featuring alongside H&M and Zara, both of which are retail chains with a distinctive type of product on offer and a specific target group. This also explains the 'normal' growth figure of 5 per cent. Although 'normal' is relative in today's market, 5 per cent growth in turnover is good in light of the current pressure on prices (and thus also on margins). The significant growth enjoyed by Primark is a result of the opening of new stores

---

10   *The Independent* (2013).

in Europe. There the concept is still a novelty and appeals to the target group, as can be seen from the hysteria that meets the opening of a store. The rise in turnover will also continue, as long as the concept continues to appeal and the choice remains limited (limited store numbers). The target group (16–34-year-olds) is fashion conscious, price conscious and sensitive to hype.

Through the strategy described above and a sharp focus on low pricing, Primark uses the Internet only to convey vision and image. This proved particularly important after the tragic events in Bangladesh, where a factory producing garments for Primark (among others) collapsed. Many lost their lives and there was outcry around the world. After a brief dip, Primark's turnover recovered fully and its image suffered no lasting damage. The store's website gives a clear and explicit account of Primark's ethics and commitment.

The Primark website: Who we are and what we stand for

Rana-Plaza long-term compensation

Primark has paid over $12 million in aid and compensation to support the victims of the Rana Plaza building, which collapsed in April 2013, tragically killing over a thousand workers. The building housed several factories, one of which produced Primark garments.

We work with specialized suppliers

Like many other clothing brands, Primark does not own the factories that make its products. We work with around 700 suppliers – from countries such as China, India and Bangladesh to Turkey and Eastern Europe. Most of these factories also make clothing for other retail chains too, and in some cases even for expensive brands!

The decision not to sell online has been a clear one for Primark. It would have gone against the low-price image and deliberate scarcity of its shops to do so. The focus is on the stores themselves and emphasises their 'hedonic' aspects. An important trump card for sales is emotional shopping, which can generate a good deal of impulse buying. Customers feel as though they are in a fantasy world of low prices and attractive modern clothing. Internet is secondary within this strategy and is therefore used only to communicate the Primark message and to respond to negative news.

Primark is one of only a few retailers not to sell through its website, as experts insist its low-cost, high-volume business model wouldn't work online. Its trademark carrier bags are made of brown paper. Store owners take pride in their shop's interior: exposed brickwork, video walls and daring window displays are common features.

Richard Perks, retail analyst at Mintel, says its success shows our fondness for 'cheap, disposable fashion. They've hit the mood perfectly. In times like these, fashionable merchandise is an affordable treat.'

Fashionistas, too, love Primark (of, as they fondly call it, «Primarni»). The chain claims it can take 'as little as six weeks' for styles from the catwalk to appear in shops.[11]

Mediamarkt

Mediamarkt is an enormous electronics shop and belongs to one of the largest retailers in Europe, Metrogroup. The stores are large, with a full array of products on offer. Everything can be looked at and tried out. In addition to its massive size and the chance to try things, the sales staff is very helpful. This experience-based shop appeals mainly to men who find inspiration in electronics. Its clever location strategy is focused on accessibility, often in city centres. In many cases a shop has underground parking facilities. This allows for optimal accessibility, and the distance to the shop and back to the car is very short. These features make Mediamarkt an important draw in shopping precincts. Men like to go there to browse and see whether there is anything new. The buying threshold is very low thanks to the wide range of products and the sense of inspiration and sensation that surrounds them. Women seem less inspired by the store and tend in any case not to buy electronics for inventive or emotional reasons, but more out of practical considerations. For them, the Internet offers many advantages.

In addition to the location policy, Mediamarkt used an aggressive marketing campaign based on price perception. Low prices, aggressive adverts with the slogan 'I'm not daft' and long opening hours (from 10 am to 10 pm and where possible on Sundays) have ensured that Mediamarkt is seen by other electronics shops as an aggressive competitor. Initially, the electronics megastore had a sharp focus on the shop floor and the shopping experience. The organisation favoured a local approach. Local managers are entrepreneurs with the freedom locally to adapt the products on offer, define their own pricing strategy and

---

11 *Daily Telegraph* (2013).

profit from local performance. This localised approach, linked to a central focus on stores, was not a natural fit for the online experience.

In 2014 the strategy was changed. In addition to the existing focus on stores, a strategy was also developed for the Internet. To this end, the organisation had to involve local managers in the development of its website and the local strategy had to be adjusted to a centralised one. The previously localised pricing policies were no longer possible if the same items were also going to be available via the Internet. A decision was thus made to feature local stores even more strongly by combining Mediamarkt stores with Saturn retail stores. The two labels were merged into a single Mediamarkt store in 2014. The result was a stronger focus on the local stores, since there were now fewer of them. The re-focus on store locations was a logical consequence of this change in strategy. In addition, agreements had to be reached with local management with regard to Internet strategy and remuneration structure.

Since 2014, Mediamarkt has become a major player on the Internet as well, but the Internet has in turn been closely integrated into stores. Member of the sales team have tablets so that they can access the right information immediately and are able to conclude a sale online. The sales staff can sell both online and in the shop, and in due course it will be possible for the salesperson to perform the entire sales process (with cash register function).

On the Internet, prices can be changed quickly to adapt to market conditions. With the introduction of digital price labels in the shop, all prices can be changed centrally at the same time. This not only allows for an efficient response to the changes, but for greater effectiveness and competitiveness. The physical shop remains important, but it is being reinforced by the application of Internet technologies, while the Internet has become an important supporting sales channel for shops. Mediamarkt is thus following the same process as that of A&F (Abercrombie & Fitch) and the expected growth phases of other retail chains.

Emotion as a Basis for Shops

For emotional shopping, location and product are very important. For a moment you can imagine yourself to be in another, luxury world – your very own dream world. By making a purchase you reward yourself, while also enhancing social cohesion – the sense of being part of a special, privileged group. Emotional, hedonic motives are the basis for this type of shopping. Moreover, with branded products, you mark out your identity and can distinguish yourself from friends and acquaintances. Shops play an important role here with their product presentation, shop design and ambiance. Flagship stores of established bands are in fact 'emotion shops', where experience and inspiration are central. It is not so much about selling, but about the image being projected, the dream world and the product association. Once you have experienced the ambiance of an Apple store, you will never forget it. The same is true of other brands such as Burberry on Regent Street, the Nike store or the Rolex shop. The feeling and experience remains with you and is reinforced by a visit to Saks Fifth Avenue or Harrods. The same sort of feeling is also generated when you visit the websites of these stores. Their sites are recognisably an extension of the shop's distinctive feeling, and vice versa. Emotion, experience and feeling are the dominant elements that produce added value. In addition, social cohesion is very important, since customers feel very special when they wear the branded item or when shopping in one of these stores. They know they belong to a special group and they show it by behaving accordingly. It is precisely the top-of-the-line brands that will have a strong presence, with flagship stores and shops being required to meet stringent image guidelines so as to uphold brand value and associations.

It is, after all, hedonic shopping that leads to a visit to a physical shop and that requires a distinctive approach to shops and shopping precincts. With this type of shopping it is not the ability to buy items that matters, but the total experience. In particular, the notion that a shop needs to project a sort of dream world, an escape from daily reality, should serve as the starting point for shops and shopping precincts. This can only succeed if all parties work together: the municipalities responsible for the public space, the first touch point for visitors; then, the property owner or owner of the shopping centre – the second touch point; the shop itself is the third touch point, and personal service could be considered the fourth touch point. Each touch point represents either a stimulus to buy or a disappointment that can lead to an 'emotional breach'. If you set out on a shopping trip and can't find a parking space, or the road is full of litter or loitering youths, you feel discouraged. If a shopping precinct or mall is dirty, outmoded, poorly lit and with many empty shops, customers may be disappointed. A shopping mall that looks ugly from the outside will not entice shoppers to go inside – flaking paint, dirty windows, a pavement that has not been swept or a shop door that is closed. Staff standing around in front of a shop smoking is a poor image if you want to attract customers. All these aspects can turn shoppers off. Inside the shop as well, attention needs to be paid to the hedonic aspects. From the way the items are displayed down to a cosy feeling and hospitality. Lighting is also important. Mood lighting, the use of colours and soft music can be a far better stimulus to buy than harsh neon lights, with no music or loud music (with the exception of shops catering for young people, where the music can be loud). It is an organic process, in which all parties have to cooperate in order to create a dream world for visitors/customers. Naturally, this also includes hospitable and well informed staff! It is a complete package in which all these elements *work together* to make real shopping fun again.

Cities with a historic centre have a clear advantage when it comes to atmosphere and experience. They often have cute little shops that still give pride of place to handmade products. Visitors go there for the experience, but they also buy! Ultimately, this is the origin of physical shopping. This type of shopping precinct grew organically, but municipalities later began to intervene with regulations to encourage concentrations of shops. In the beginning, this was done with a view to retaining control, but nowadays there are other motives, with less favourable consequences to retailers (for example, land on a statement of financial position that must be transferred or sold to project developers).

Hedonic Shops

Besides Primark, there are other shops that place experience at the centre in order to motivate customers. In many cases, technology can be part of this, as we shall see later, but it is not indispensable. We all know a local shop or café where you particularly enjoy shopping because of the atmosphere or the service. Larger stores can also pursue a distinctive concept. Harrods[12] in London is an experience store, drawing visitors from around the world who are inspired by the shop, the merchandise and the service. Primark has found a unique combination to attract and motivate customers, a strong focus on its target group and a sense of scarcity in combination with low prices.

Abercrombie & Fitch decided to take a special approach to young people. A restrictive admission policy to the shop meant that there was always a queue of people waiting outside the door. Attractive men at the entrance entertained them while they waited, suggesting a wonderful, carefree life style. Inside,

---

12 Harrods is a department store on the Brompton Road in Knightsbridge, London, specialising in luxury goods. In addition to the department store, the Harrods Company also includes a bank, an estate agent and an airline.

the shop features accent lighting directed onto the clothing collection, leaving the shop and aisles in darkness. Interesting little spaces and music chosen specially for the target group and the merchandise, with different music in each department makes for a sort of disco feel and turns the shopping experience into something special.

When A&F shops were first introduced, the concept was a completely innovative one, but over the years it has become a bit tired. Today, the stores have become more mainstream. What was once special and unique has now become normal. Queues at the door are now rare. In the early years it was almost impossible to buy A&F products online. Delivery outside the United States was often impossible, and later the shipping and handling costs in particular were kept very high. Through these measures, buying online was discouraged. Now that A&F has become more mainstream, everything can be bought online with free shipping. The Internet is also used by A&F to convey inspiration and 'experience'. A link with Instagram is part of this. Perhaps this development is just a trend: first, make the store special and focus all marketing activities on the shop (as Primark and A&F did in the beginning). Then, and only once the concept begins to wear, should you launch a webshop in order to compensate for falling turnover in the shops.

Other elements that initially contributed to making A&F successful are being modified in order to meet customers' changing desires and do something about declining sales. Thus A&F began to sell black clothing items for the first time. Music in the shops was turned down and daylight was allowed in. These changes were first made in the United States, since the buzz there had come to an end. When the hype wanes, selling comes to occupy a more central place and the Internet begins to play a supporting role; perhaps gaining the edge over physical shops at a later date. This is a clear development.

Groceries

The vast majority of consumers do not want to order groceries online, even if their primary supermarket offers this service. This was the result of the 2014 Consumer trends study conducted by Flycatcher on behalf of Deloitte among 2400 consumers.

> *Of those surveyed, 85 per cent of the shoppers said they do not use this service. The respondents also said they would not choose the web shop of*

another supermarket. In 2013 that figure was 82 per cent. Consumers who never order groceries online give as the principal reason that they want to see or select the produce. And they would prefer not to have to pay delivery costs.[13]

The effect of the Internet on grocery shopping behaviour (at supermarkets) is still modest. There appears to be a strong preference to buy such items in person, daily if one has the time, weekly for bigger shops. Thanks to extended supermarket opening hours, there are almost no restrictions. People can shop any time, even on Sundays. Resorting to the Internet for grocery shopping due to a lack of time is therefore usually not a valid motive. Finally, with groceries there is no need to buy online because a given item is not available in your area. What is more, nearly all supermarkets in recent years have undergone a facelift, both in the shop itself and in the product assortment – in terms of both quality and quantity (particularly of fresh foods).

New figures from Kantar Worldpanel show grocery sales rose just 0.8pc in the 12 weeks to 17 August [2014], the slowest pace for a decade, with even the seemingly resilient] Sainsbury suffering. The slowdown is being caused by price deflation as supermarkets cut prices and the discounters Aldi and Lidl grow their market share.

[Clive Black, analyst at Shore Capital] added: 'Consumer behaviour in the UK is changing with households still carefully managing their budgets. Whilst employment levels are high, living standards are growing at a very pedestrian rate and groceries have been a key lever in managing down household budgets.

Such a lever has positioned the limited assortment discounters and high street value retailers very well for the prevailing mood. Additionally though, an increasing number of folk are eating out more, where value can be strong in pubs and cafés, plus the affordable treat remains a robust feature of spending patterns'.[14]

And yet clear changes can be seen in the grocery channel. These changes affect competition among supermarkets, competition among brands for customer preference, competition for shelf space and the changes brought about by a sharp focus on costs within the channel.

---

13 Retailnieuws.nl, 29 August 2014.

14 *Daily Telegraph* (2014a).

> *While the proportion of groceries sold online is much smaller than other sectors, the vast size of the food market means it is a key avenue of growth for under-pressure mainline supermarkets. Stuart Rose, chairman of Ocado, told the Guardian that the online grocery market had reached the 'point of inflection'. 'The future for online food retail is very exciting. We are at the beginning of a revolution and the pace of change is accelerating. It's online showtime', he said.*[15]

The developments in technology and their impact on consumers were ignored for a very long time by fast-moving consumer goods companies (FMCG). Marketing did not change, in spite of the fact that customers were reading fewer newspapers, watching less TV and had more choices via the Internet. Marketers stuck firmly to the mass media, even though the impact of these has fallen dramatically in recent years. Social media, mobile phones and the Internet have to date remained a struggle for FMCG and for supermarkets. Whereas other sectors went in search of this new consumer – with music, travel and fashion taking the lead – the food sector kept its head in the sand. Consumer spending will not rise in the coming years, but there will be a shift in the allocation of disposable income. An increasing portion will be spent on electronics and related items (now between 7 and 9 per cent of the budget). This may be on items such as a digital television, apps, games or a new iPhone 6. Because disposable income is not rising, savings have to be made elsewhere, and that somewhere would appear to be groceries. Shopping at Lidl is much cheaper than at Tesco and a store brand is cheaper than a brand name item. This shift is having a significant impact on the position of the market leader, as well as on branded items. The increase in spend on technology indicates that the competition is now no longer coming from other supermarkets, but from different spending patterns. Competition is increasingly taking place at a spend level: a new iPhone, mobile subscription and online games are fighting for a greater share of the budget. If one can spend less on groceries, more will be available to spend on these products. The awareness that there might be another recession, with consequences for the household budget (and mortgage costs) is prompting caution among consumers.

Another potential cause of FMCG problems is the rigidity of the sector. Negotiations are constantly being conducted about yet another low price. The structure is hierarchical, cooperation is rare. Manufacturers must sell in order to get their products on the shelves, while supermarkets want to devote increasingly less space to branded goods, privileging their own brands. Tough

---

15   *The Guardian* (2014a).

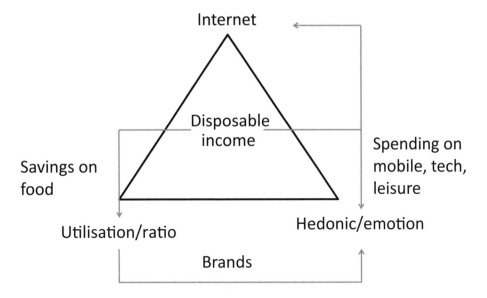

Figure 4.2   A change in free disposable income

negotiations around conditions and margins are the consequence, with distrust all around.

These are only the areas which have received publicity, but they clearly point to tensions in the food channel and this is hardly a good foundation for cooperation and innovation. The need for renewal and innovation will be felt in the short term, but both the financial backing and involvement levels are lacking. Under these circumstances, we see opportunities for no-frills shops with a limited offering and low prices to step in to fill the gap. Thanks to a strong focus on quality, especially of fresh produce, a change is occurring in the marketplace. Customers can see the (financial) advantage of shopping at these stores and are doing so increasingly, causing the major players to lose market share. Cutting price alone, certainly to the level of the no-frills stores, is not sufficient.

> *Edward Garner, director of Kantar Worldpanel, said that Asda and Waitrose had achieved their market growth with very different strategies: "Asda has pushed its 'price lock' strategy to keep prices on everyday essential items low, while Waitrose is running competitive offers on home delivery alongside offers for myWaitrose card users allied to its overall quality and provenance positioning.*

Waitrose's strong pace of growth meant it managed to hold off Aldi which hovers just 0.1 percentage point away from drawing level as the UK's sixth largest grocer, according to Kantar."

Rival market analysts Nielsen say Aldi has already overtaken Waitrose.

Supermarket shares, 12 weeks to 17 August 2014

- *Tesco 28.8%*
- *Asda 17.2%*
- *Sainsbury's 16.4%*
- *Morrisons 11%*
- *Co-operative 6.4%*
- *Waitrose 4.9%*
- *Aldi 4.8%*
- *Lidl 3.6%*
- *Iceland 2%*

Source: Kantar.[16]

What Does the New Buying Behaviour Mean for Supermarkets

The sharp rise of Lidl and Aldi is an international phenomenon. Market leaders such as Tesco and Sainsbury's are avidly searching for new, innovative solutions. Tesco installed a QR wall at Heathrow Airport so that holidaymakers could place an order with their mobile phones before departing. Upon their return, the items purchased were ready for pick-up. The initiative was a flop.

Since the recession, British families, like their Dutch counterparts, have been more careful with their spending. Instead of simply jumping into the car each week and driving to an 'out-of-town' supermarket for the weekly shop, customers now tend to buy less each time, but shop more frequently. There is also much more switching between different supermarkets. Some families buy the basics from discount stores or online, then go to their local supermarket on their way home from work to pick up fresh produce and smaller items.

Consumers are increasingly prepared to discover new options, with the discounters Aldi and Lidl the big winners in this regard, along with the upmarket Waitrose, on account of the quality of their fresh food items. Eating

---

16   *The Guardian* (2014b).

out is also popular, as are ready meals. Any savings are then put towards the occasional treat or small indulgence.

This has given rise to what some analysts are calling a 'perfect storm' for greengrocers and supermarkets. Based on the current trend, within five years 'out-of-town' supermarkets will account for a smaller share of food sales than all the discounters, online shops and convenience stores taken together. That is a significant shift in the market, one that the 'big four' (with Tesco at the head) must address.[17] All sorts of innovations among supermarkets have not hitherto yielded the desired result for market leaders.[18] Experiments with online sales have not produced a breakthrough. Tesco has opted to expand its non-food Internet offering. The Tesco brand name and the proximity of its shops have made this possible. Tesco also has an advanced club card system, which customers can use to save up for vouchers. The vouchers can be used for discounts as well as for free entry to amusement parks or cultural events. Finally, Tesco is trying to gain customer loyalty by using communities and clubs of similar categories of customers. But there is also a certain fatigue among the British with Tesco. Customers would like something different once in a while. And so new and promising concepts are tried out. Attempting to follow the constant innovations and technological changes can also lead to a degree of fatigue among customers. Thus we see a return to the basics, which have again become trendy, like Lidl, Asda and similar discount shops.

In August 2014 Tesco appointed a new CEO after recent changes had not proven successful. The new Harris+Hoole coffee shops and Giraffe restaurants in the supermarkets did not stop customers leaving for Aldi or Lidl. Urgent advice to reduce prices was not followed. The new CEO was given a budget of £750 million to take whatever measures were necessary to staunch the outflow of customers. The money came from retained dividends, and at the same time a promise was made that more money would be made available if necessary. The new CEO will have to act quickly and boldly to stop the current trend and to ensure that shareholders and customers alike are satisfied. A huge challenge!

Tesco hopes to be a clear leader in innovation and thereby to win customers' loyalty. Whether they will succeed in doing so remains to be seen. Competition for customers in the UK is fierce. It amounts to a price war. Sainsbury's, a major rival of Tesco, has been trying to reverse its declining earnings by not opening any new stores, by selling more via the Internet, and by lowering prices as far

---

17 Based on an analysis by Graham Ruddick in the *Daily Telegraph* (2014b).
18 YouTube (2012a).

as possible. The non-food product range available online, including clothing, is expected to contribute in particular to greater sales. Mike Coupe, CEO of Sainsbury's, talks about an 'all hands on deck' approach to targeting customers' new buying behaviour and to counter the popularity of discounters such as Aldi and Lidl.[19]

Changes are also afoot when it comes to policy regarding locations. All supermarkets want smaller shops, closer to the customer. Options on sites outside residential areas are being surrendered. The major supermarkets have already sustained hundreds of millions in losses. A similar pattern can also be observed in France, where Carrefour is looking at having fewer hypermarkets and more supermarkets in residential neighbourhoods. This means that the array of products can be better customised to local needs, and the shops are also conveniently located so that customers can shop more often. As a result, the need for online shopping is falling. This is thought to be advantageous for shops, since online shopping orders and home delivery drive up costs at the supermarkets operating in a sector which aims for ever lower costs. Furthermore, the loyalty of a shopper who regularly visits the same shop is greater than that of the online customer. Blindly assuming that the Internet is the solution to the current competition among supermarkets is naïve. Supermarkets can easily copy each other's strategies. Soon there will be no more competitive advantage to be achieved, and the Internet will only lead to higher costs. The strategy of Lidl and other discount stores to focus on costs is not such a bad thing. The struggle is more and more about the customer and the latter's motives and loyalty. Product offering, service, price and location will once again be the decisive factors for supermarkets.

Migros is a popular chain of supermarkets in Switzerland, and the smaller 'Migrolinos', in particular, are highly successful. These are small supermarkets located in residential areas and at petrol stations. The prices are higher than at the big supermarkets, but that matters little when offset by speed and convenience. After all, in the large shops where prices are deliberately kept low, people do buy expensive cigarettes and fine wines as well. The traditional target groups have disappeared. Customers drive up to a shop in a BMW to buy cheap shampoo and toilet paper, but then also buy expensive wines (for 300 Swiss Francs). Shoppers want to save on the essentials but not on luxury items. Migros attributes its success to two factors. One: you can no longer rely on traditional target group structures, profiles and shopping preferences. Two: the customer's state of mind; people always want a fair deal, the sense that they

---

19 *Daily Telegraph* (2014c).

have not paid over the odds for something. That is why the image of a cheap supermarket is important, so you can save on the basic products in order to be able to treat yourself with the occasional fancy cigar and a bottle of fine wine. A 'feel good' factor, since the customer is sure to have got value for his/her money. According to Migros, it's not on price that you need to compete, but on offering a fair deal.[20]

Brands

Supermarkets aren't the only ones to have to adapt to the new consumer. Manufacturers of fast-moving consumer goods do as well. Branded goods face a few problems when it comes to today's consumers.[21] Consumers shop differently and have different reasons for buying than did previous generations. Firstly, customers today always want to have the very latest product, and so every innovation must offer something distinctive. This generation is extremely well informed and can see right through advertising bumph. Secondly, FMCG retailers don't know their customers and do not build loyalty. A third reason is that investment in R&D is essential in order to continue to remain distinctive. If that fails, a price war is the consequence, with a dramatic impact on profit margins. The final reason is that most products are so highly developed that only minor adjustments are still possible. Such small changes do not make a great impression on today's consumer. What we are seeing is a series of changes that follow one another in rapid succession and are clearly recognisable to the customer. Apple is a prime example of this. The core issue is how to be noticed and how to earn customer loyalty. Since FMCG companies are not familiar with their customers and not in a position to create a bond with them, the challenge is great. Pressure on disposable income also plays a role here, so that cheap 'brands', particularly own brands, are gaining market share.

Change is the Only Way to Respond to the New Customer Behaviour

Consumers buy differently than in the past, and if shops continue doing what they have always done, this will inevitably lead to disappointment. Even preserving the old by prohibiting innovations in shopping precincts and town centres, as is now being proposed, is to deny what customers want. If shoppers

---

20 Lorange and Rembiszewski (2014), p. 24.
21 Lorange and Rembiszewski (2014), pp. 68ff.

see no added value in shops, the trend will simply intensify, as customers simply turn to the Internet or go to different locations to shop. What is needed is a vision of the future that understands what role shops could play in the new buying process. That will certainly mean different kinds of shops and a new kind of retail landscape, with altered roles for manufacturers, suppliers and shops.

Town centres will also undergo change, but that is in any case an on-going process. For decades, customers were discouraged from going to shop in the town centre because of environmental pressures, the trucks needed to supply the shops, limited opening hours and a ban on street furniture, poor air quality on account of car traffic and noise pollution. Why should the shops in the town centre now suddenly be saved? Shops will continue to exist, in a different form perhaps and with different values, but at locations that are meaningful to their customers – with experiences, inspiration and entertainment, all at locations that are easily accessible by bike, car and public transport. That being said, the driverless car is on its way and so the entire transport system to city centres, including car parks and paid parking, may be on its last legs. City centres will change: culture, small specialty boutiques and eateries will be important. A compact city centre will be a nice place to take a stroll. Just like those favourite holiday spots we like to stroll down.

Chapter 5

What Choices Do We Have?

It would appear that customers are becoming ever more critical. Before they make purchases, they first have a thorough look on the Internet. They Google the product, read the accompanying information, compare prices, read customer reviews and perhaps look proactively for reactions on Twitter, Facebook or Pinterest. The future customer has many options. Loaded with knowledge, information and preferences, they go to the shops in search of the item, (sometimes) have a chat with the sales staff before deciding to buy. But why would you look for the item in the shops if it can be found just as easily online? Shops are now being used to check if the choice already made is the right one (show rooming). Shopping areas are no longer attractive enough for customers to choose expressly and to visit them. So how can retailers still draw people in and cultivate customer loyalty to shops and shopping precincts? Buying behaviour provides a clear indication of where the opportunities lie. Customers nowadays make a conscious choice as to how and where they want to shop. In the process of making their choice, they are open to suggestions (reason) and feelings (emotion/hedonic). How can a retailer influence that process today, and what factors are key to the consumer's decision-making process? Although it would be handy to identify universal steps in a buying process, it is often simply a matter of individual choice: online or offline, from a local shop, at a mall or somewhere else.

Will it be a Local Shopping Centre, a Central Mall or Town?

In the physical world, the choice to be made involves the location and the shop. Travelling distance and accessibility are very important. The shopping centre or precinct has to be able to attract customers with its atmosphere, varied offering and, naturally, ease of access. If visitors feel positively about a given spot, shops need to play into that. Harmony is very important here – shops of a similar quality, with sufficient diversity, bring in a homogeneous public. The shops at certain parts of a shopping street share a degree of homogeneity, thus attracting similar types of customers. Consumers want not only homogeneity but also diversity in the range of shops; their choice is determined not only by what the shops offer but also by the time available. If the customer has little time he or she may prefer to shop close to home, but if time is not an issue, they might make a different choice. In that case, the hedonic (emotional) factors are important, such as pleasure, relaxation and a chance to get away from the daily grind, routine or stress of daily life. The difference between these two types of shopping has a decisive effect on what shops offer. Local shops, where you can get your shopping done fast, are important for the daily grocery run. At large shopping centres, the overall experience plays a more significant role. A study conducted by Matthew Collum[1] indicates that relaxation is an important factor in opting for larger centres, along with accessibility and parking facilities. His research showed that when choosing the place to shop, customers were not influenced so much by higher petrol costs, but rather by the cost of parking. The reason for this is probably that the parking cost was associated directly with buying at that particular location, whereas the petrol price was not factored into the shopping itself.

Quite apart from these secondary reasons (parking), the shopping centre itself must be appealing in terms of the quality and diversity of shops, food outlets and services. The presence of 'anchor stores' in particular, such as we see in England: Debenhams, John Lewis and Selfridges in large malls and Marks & Spencer in smaller centres are important factors in attracting customers and developing their loyalty. Large centres will have different 'anchor stores', such as Zara, H&M and well-known fashion shops. In the UK research, Primark was not mentioned. Our earlier analysis showed that Primark is no longer hyped in England, but is simply 'business as usual' for a specific target group. The eating options available are often cited as important: a sushi restaurant, Asian cuisine or the environment as a whole. Ultimately, it is always a question of choosing between buying and pleasure, between spending time and shopping efficiently. Naturally there are differences based on personal circumstances, as previously mentioned, but it would be oversimplifying to refer only to those. A shopping centre and a shop must simply be attractive and magnetic.

These days, however, it is no longer simply a choice of which shopping centre or which shop to buy from, but also whether to buy from a shop at all. Here, too, personal factors such as time, affinity and the desire for a brief escape from the daily grind and reality have an important role to play.

---

1   Collum (2013).

Why Buy Online?

The reason people buy online is often personal. It may be due to impulse, a 'feel-good' moment, a result of curiosity, or it could be a perfectly rational and goal-oriented decision. There is a clear distinction to be made between goal-oriented (or rational) and emotional (hedonic) buying. This goes for the physical store as well as for online, except the possible choices are more numerous and the speed of the transaction much faster online. The most important reasons for buying online are convenience and reason. Thanks to greater knowledge, gained by data analysis and the use of the latest technological possibilities, hedonic aspects of online buying behaviour are steadily gaining importance. More purchases are being made per visit, and buyers will probably return sooner and more often. This interaction is significant, since retailers can try to influence it, whereas physical shops fail to pick up on it. Shops have no knowledge of their customers and analyses are based purely on turnover (product sales), rather than the customers themselves.

Customers who visit webshops can also be divided into two categories. One group merely browses and enjoys doing so, going in search of inspiration, information and experience. This group visits websites that are attractive, novel and clearly gives priority to the fun factor. Besides layout, colour palettes and attractive photography, videos often feature too. These websites exude pleasure and glamour. This often applies to websites of high-end brands and quality shops. This group goes for inspiration, association and fun, not so much with a view to buying. The other group of users, on the other hand, surf the net precisely in order to buy – these are the rational visitors. They surf with a particular goal: to buy quickly and efficiently. These discoveries have led the researcher Daniele Scarpi[2] to the conclusion that there is a dichotomy among the visitors to a website, just as there is among those who frequent shops. Browsers or buyers. A striking conclusion of the study is the role of price. In physical shopping, there is certainly a difference in price association between fun shoppers and rational shoppers, but this difference is not evident on the Internet. This means that the hedonic Internet user, in search of inspiration and fun, is also price-conscious. Price can be seen as an important motive for buying online for every visitor. There is a clear distinction in loyalty (return shopping), however. The rational buyers are so focused on price that they have no specific intention to come back, whereas the fun visitors will, assuming they have had a positive experience, choose deliberately to return. After a positive association, or 'inspirience', a fun visitor will become a loyal visitor.

---

2 Scarpi (2012).

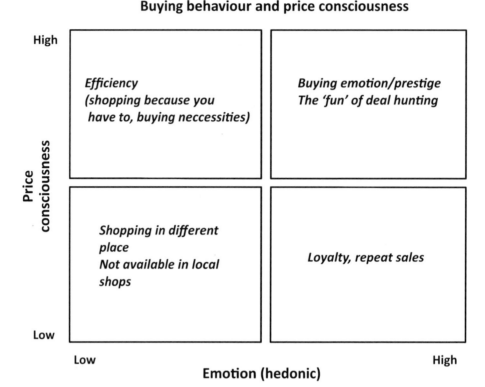

Buying behaviour and price consciousness

Figure 5.1   Prices are especially important for low emotion products/ ratio shopping

Such visitors will return more often and will make more frequent purchases in order to regain the sense of joy they felt first time around. For this reason, the hedonic customer is a more valuable and more profitable one than a customer guided mainly by reason. The former will buy more often, buy more and go with the good feeling. In contrast, a decision based on price alone is a rational one, deprived of emotion.

Scarpi's study also investigated the demographic and gender differences among shoppers, across all product categories combined. The research identified no difference between the sexes or between young and old. This means that hedonic shopping online, alongside rational shopping, occurs among both young and old, both men and women. This is a universal behaviour. The difference between the hedonic and rational groups does, however, impact the purchasing and browsing behaviour and is therefore something for retailers or shopkeepers who also have an Internet presence, to take into account.

Visitors who buy for rational motives spend less time online per visit (speed is important) than do 'hedonic' visitors.

Is There a Difference between Web Shopping and Physical Shopping?

Web shopping is sometimes seen as complementary to going to the shops. In the case of the new, hybrid concept, it has been proposed that web shopping can be a support to physical shopping. In the previous chapters we have seen that emotional factors are particularly important when it comes to shopping at physical stores. A significant portion of stores are fashion/clothing shops. Shoppers there are guided not solely by reason, but particularly by emotion and loyalty. It would therefore be reasonable to conclude that web shopping is something entirely different and that the motives for online shopping therefore also differ from motives for physical shopping. A comparison of the two – Internet and physical shops – suggests that this is not so. In the diagram above, a correlation is made between emotion and price-consciousness. This relationship is based on a study of fashion shoppers.[3] There is a group of buyers who purchase online only because it is cheaper, or conversely who buy offline because it is cheaper. This group of customers can be found at Primark and Action, as we have seen above. Price is the dominant factor when making a purchase, and a change in price will immediately have a negative effect on buying. This category of buyers is the rational shoppers, who buy when there is a need, not so much for the sake of the experience or because shopping is fun. Shopping for them is a necessity for functional purposes. The price must therefore be proportionate to the efficiency of the channel and the range of products on offer at the webshop or the physical shop.

Online shops have a strong advantage with regard to these customers, since price comparison can be done more easily and better online. These customers will often turn to the Internet simply for convenience and efficiency. Where there is a strong relationship between price-consciousness and functional necessity, in other words, absence of emotion, online shopping will be the channel of choice. That is why it was this consumer group that was the first to be drawn to the Internet. Retailers still foster the image that the Internet is cheaper. If this is the case, cheapness only represents a strong motive for the price-conscious buyer who shops out of necessity. In this case, the buyer makes a deliberate choice, weighing up the pros and cons of buying in a physical shop versus buying online. The customer simply wants to be done as fast as possible.

---

3   Scarpi, Pizzi and Visentin (2014).

The aim is efficiency, albeit with a sense of having bought at a good price. In this regard, the perception of the shop in question plays a major role. Action is always cheap, and so is Lidl. Branding is thus important in aligning perception with reality. When it comes to shopping out of necessity, the key considerations are thus efficiency at the lowest price. With other purchases too, price can be important for hedonism: the thrill of bargaining, searching for the lowest price, getting the best deal. Customers want to be able to compare prices, and the best place to do that is on the Internet. Hence Internet shoppers are much more price conscious in their buying than those who shop in physical stores.[4]

Online Shopping Out of Necessity

In some cases, there is no question of choice. Certain items are simply not available to purchase locally. The Internet then becomes the only solution. This can happen for items for which there is little local demand, items that are specific to a region or country, or where there are restrictions on a product (it may be that there is no importer for the product in that country, for example). This can apply to food products, for instance, products that cater for food allergies. For these types of products there may be little or no local supply available, whereas online there are many providers thanks to the economies of scale. Customers have no other choice, in such cases, than to buy online; we are dealing with what can be referred to as a functional necessity, rather than with emotion, and price-consciousness has little or no role.

When emotion is involved, price-consciousness will in principle be less significant. Where people compare prices, this is always on the same item, and not between different items. This is not so much because of a limited budget or a need to buy for the lowest price, but because bargain hunting is almost a kind of sport. Can I find this item somewhere for less? Ironically, these are often the most expensive items a customer will purchase, and the decision as to where to buy them is based on price!

The final factor considered in the diagram is emotional buyers who attach little importance to price. Emotion or inspiration is important, perhaps more so even than the product itself. Here we will see loyalty to a store, a webshop or a brand. Positive past experiences can also play an important role. Thanks to this positive experience (such as service, delivery, trust), a client will come back and will consider the price in relation to other aspects. This behaviour indicates the

---

4   Scarpi, Pizzi and Visentin (2014).

importance of after-care/customer service. Later I will return to this question when considering loyalty.

The study cited above concluded that the online context is nevertheless more complicated than the offline context. When shopping offline, location and the selection of products on offer are often important criteria, as is personal contact, while online these factors have negligible impact. Online, the experience while shopping (browsing) plays an important role – this includes the layout and the overall image of the site, as well as recommendations from others. Social media has an increasingly important place in the pre-shopping experience. Facebook for one, thanks to the opportunity to share experiences among friends and acquaintances. But customer reviews on the vendor's website can also be a motivator or de-motivator. In the physical world, fun shopping is more common than in the online world. It is precisely the physical experience and the hedonic aspects which we have already discussed – such as excitement and going out – which have a significant influence on the buying experience. With online shopping, price always plays a role, but is weighed up against the entire buying process. Slow websites, poor layout, complex payment conditions can all serve as de-motivators, notwithstanding a lower price.

The difference between online and offline is actually smaller than it was previously. Price has become increasingly important for both shops and webshops, but interestingly a growing group of buyers are heading to the Internet for explanations and information. Webshops take advantage of this by disseminating information via video, for example, and seek to strike a balance between emotion and reason. Physical shops should also seek the same balance, both in terms of product offering and store layout and design. Achieving this equilibrium demands careful judgement from all parties. The last thing you want to do is alienate your customer from your concept. In this respect, webshops perhaps have an easier job as they have the means to communicate before, during and following the purchase. Communication need not be limited to email, but can be done via affiliate websites or social media.

Shops need passers-by. Through good integration with Internet (the hybrid concept) there are sound opportunities for new store concepts. Providers (shops) must decide what to focus on: fun or price, utility (rationalism) or hedonism (emotion). The customer is then left to choose the channel (online or offline) or a concept (supporting behaviour). This clearly illustrates the confusion today's shoppers feel in the High Street. People are shopping in the name of enjoyment and escapism from the daily grind, but all shops can do for them is offer discounts. Huge signs with 50%, 60% or 70% discounts do not match up with customers' expectations. What they are offering is not an emotive shopping experience, but a 'good deal'. And the place for good deals is the Internet. Surprise, inspiration and motivation are what belong on the High Street! Yet High Streets all over the country are completely identical and dominated by the large retail chains. It is the small, independent shops and hospitality that create atmosphere and a unique product offering. Yet high rental fees keep this type of shop away from A1 locations. No wonder that fewer and fewer people are visiting these places. All the emphasis is on making sales and not on the actual customers. Local activities – from Christmas lights to street fairs – require financial backing from local shop owners. More often than not, the large chain stores are denied permission from head office to participate. It's almost a form of self-punishment.

Loyalty

Attracting customers is difficult enough, but retaining them is harder still. On the Internet, much time and attention is spent on communication. But what makes customers return? What is it that binds them to a particular product, brand or shop? Customer loyalty can be split into two groups: behavioural loyalty and attitudinal loyalty. With behavioural loyalty, customers return to make repeat purchases. These are ideal customers for a shop, product and webshop alike. To cultivate this type of loyalty, you not only need a satisfied customer, but also a customer who is reassured they have made the right choice and who feels trust and security, as well as emotion and a feeling of having been rewarded on making the purchase. The other type of loyalty – attitudinal loyalty – is more grounded in emotion and feeling. It relates to the feelings a customer holds for a given shop or brand. This need not necessarily go hand-in-hand with a purchase, however. Names such as Porsche and Ferrari evoke a positive feeling in a great many people, but the market share is very limited. The same goes for Amazon.com – a name that enjoys great trust through brand recognition, but is not used by all. Amazon boasts excellent repeat custom. Recognition, trust and a good price point are the binding factors (for behavioural loyalty). Shops should take heed. Behavioural loyalty can be measured through repeat custom, which can be encouraged with appropriate (direct or email) communication. Attitudinal loyalty can also be measured: customers can be asked how satisfied they are. This involves sending an email following purchase asking for opinions, looking at customer reviews and the website's guestbook. A methodology has been developed especially to measure attitudinal loyalty, called the NPS score or 'net promoter' score. Are your customers brand ambassadors? Ask them to give you a figure following their purchase. Anything above an eight counts. Anything below a six gets deducted. Scores of eight, nine and ten are called promoters. Scores of six and under, critics. A simple addition and calculation gives you your score. The higher the score, the more satisfied the customers are, and the more likely they are to tell others. This is how attitudinal loyalty is measured. Customers have made their purchase and are satisfied. Follow-up calculations verify whether customers do indeed return. For scores over eight, this will certainly be the case. Furthermore, this group will also spread the good feedback either in person (word of mouth), or via social media. Actively following social media gives immediate insight into customer opinions – be they good or bad. This creates a group of customers who are loyal both in behaviour and attitude. Successful Internet businesses know very well how to use this method to bind customers, but also to improve service.[5]

Physical shops have more of a challenge in retaining customer loyalty. Certain acclimatisation to a physical shop seems to occur. Because shopping is often about the search for excitement and stimulation, repeated visits to the same shop somehow gradually lose this sense of suspense. As the 'dream world' flops, other hedonic values take its place, such as feeling, emotion, comfort and familiarity. Aesthetics also play a role here. Think of lighting, design and product displays. Abercrombie & Fitch is a prime example of this. During the initial years, the stores were somewhat of a spectacle to behold. The only light in the shop was spotlighting on the products themselves, whilst the aisles and cubbyholes remained in darkness, creating the impression of a maze you had to find a way out of. The queues of people at the doors only added to the excitement. But with time, excitement fades along with expectations, and before long, it was 'business as usual' for A&F. The company readjusted its concept and Abercrombie & Fitch in the United States – the home of the company – became a regular shop. Even the clothes changed. Garments clearly displaying the A&F name are now (2014) no longer in production. Attitudinal loyalty, where customers like to parade the fact that they shop at a certain store, has been replaced by behavioural loyalty. The challenge for A&F is making this switch and still attracting customers. Lighting plays a key role in the shopping experience. A&F takes this to the extreme, but lighting contributes to the atmosphere, excitement and make believe feel in any shop. It is not possible to emulate a similar experience on the Internet. The application of new technologies such as iBeacons used to direct smartphone communications,

---

5 This paragraph is partially based on research by Scarpi, Pizzi and Visentin (2014).

interactive mirrors (augmented reality), dynamic lighting that adapts to external factors such as the number of visitors, the weather, department or time of day serve to enhance the physical shopping experience.

Brand Preference

Brands have a high degree of attitudinal loyalty. They form part of dreams and expectations and create associations. A brand is often a way of communicating who or what you are or would like to be. It is to be expected that brand perception and expectations play a significant part in purchasing. This factor too is strongly linked to physical experience. High-end shops on London's Regent Street carry you off into a whole other world with their stunning displays and gorgeous products. Brands evoke emotion, with advanced advertising methods having a lot to answer for. The brands need to be able to emulate the same sensations created in their advertising campaigns, as much in the boutiques as in the warehouses. This way, physical presence will remain important. Flagship stores adhere to this strategy. The Internet contributes to the emotional aspects, that is, to attitudinal loyalty. Websites must reflect the brand feel that prevails in the stores. Online shopping doesn't cut it here. This is about escaping from reality and imagining your own ideal world, and is particularly the case for non-food brands, such as clothing brands. In contrast, foodstuffs brands were introduced in the 1950s with a view to providing customers with reissuance, and in the 1960s for direct outreach to the target audience through mass media. Neither motive applies any longer. Today, we have every faith in supplies and in inspection authorities and mass media is used increasingly less for advertising purposes. Personalised communication is what matters now. Brands do not know their customers and are not in a position to communicate with them directly. Hence the need for them to differentiate themselves in other areas, such as association and feeling. But even this may prove insufficient to bind consumers, as Peter Lorange concludes in his book, *Great to Gone*, which explains why FMCG companies will lose the race for the customer.

Choosing between Online and Offline

The dilemma facing customers is twofold: where to buy from in the physical world – which shop, shopping centre – and where to buy from – offline or online. The latter option is possible from the comfort of one's own home. Initially, customers were reluctant to buy online due to lack of knowledge of the medium, little experience of computers and the risks associated with paying over the web. In recent years, these arguments represent less of a barrier. More and more people were turning to the Internet to source information or for 'gaming'. As a result, customers became much more familiar and comfortable with both the Internet and computers. New devices such as smartphones and tablets have without question also contributed to intensive Internet uptake. We are seeing technology become more of a necessity as opposed to the luxury it once was. Smartphones have become indispensable to our way of living and communicating. Trust with regard to making Internet purchases has also grown significantly. Consumer acceptance of the medium coupled with the speed in which computer technology has evolved has allowed the Internet to mature. As such, reasons for buying online are influenced by a different set of factors (such as convenience, home delivery, low price) to the reasons for buying locally or cheaply. These rational aspects are replaced with personal reasons, such as being able to free up more time for other things, as we've seen already. This also calls for a revised approach from suppliers. In addition to the physical channel, there must also be an online proposition. Needless to say, in order to be able to devise a successful multi-channel strategy, suppliers must first be clear on what it is the customer is looking to achieve through going online, whether it's for information or to make a purchase. Multi channel does not mean dual channel whereby precisely the same items are available online as well as offline. Rather one channel supports the other through making information available on the Internet that will promote offline sales (demonstrated by brands) or the presence of a local branch to support the online proposition. It is important to monitor these customer behaviours and buying motives, as they help the retailer help the customer and are the route to attracting new customers.[6] The 'show rooming' phenomenon is a consequence of this: customers first search the web, then visit the shop, only to return to the web to make their purchase. Besides being extremely frustrating for shops, show rooming is an undeniable part of new buying behaviour.

Developments in technology act as major stimuli for Internet use and online purchasing. The market developments (dynamics) are what follow. A successful multi-channel strategy and Internet success rely on the commitment of an organisation's top management. Management need to participate in an e-commerce project and help employees solve problems. Without this level of commitment and involvement, the project will lack adequate support and leadership decisions will be made without consideration for and knowledge

---

6   The conclusions are the result of a study by Al-Majali and Prigmore (2010).

of Internet buying behaviour. The requisites for e-commerce success are: accurate, complete and detailed information that is evidence backed, an efficient web-based transaction process and response to customer behaviour and customer queries – both on the website in question and on social media.[7]

The Customer Purchasing Process

We have already seen that shopping is led by emotion and that there are three phases to the process. When buying necessities, these phases are born out of a 'need' and closely tied to the use and consumption of the items in question. Hence why such purchases are labelled rational (utilitarian). Habit plays an important role, as do efficiency and price. The role of technology is still limited, with existing applications aimed at supporting the purchasing process at the shop. Here, we see the three phases described in part one of this book in practice: Efficiency, effectiveness and disruption. There is efficiency in the cash register system, self-scanning and digital price tags; effectiveness in automated inventory management automated orders and disruption at the moment a new concept is introduced. At present, this is still only happening on a small scale. (We will return to this point later.) What is important for this buying process is support.

Other factors steer the process of buying occasional items. These include age, wealth, social mobility[8] and family status. Although influential, these parameters are less crucial than the reasons *why* customers buy. In other words, knowledge of why customers buy in the way that they do, is key.[9] The Internet is significant for customer orientation, i.e. in their researching a product before and during the buying phase. But its use extends to after-sales too. Customer service, social media and customer reviews demonstrate this clearly. Technology, as in the Internet in particular, is the major 'disruptor' in the purchasing process.

Choices are made more quickly on the Internet thanks to the speed in which information can be sought and retrieved. Personal motives for searching for particular information and a particular product are what implicate the Internet as part of the buying process. The decision as to where the final purchase will

7   Jantarajaturapath and Ussahawanitchkit (2009).
8   Molenaar (2013).
9   Lambin (2008), p. 94.

eventually be made is personal. The decision may based on a number of factors, including those listed below:[10]

> *Value for money,* meaning the relationship between the cost of a product and the advantage it affords. Value for money may be physical, imagined (an experience or brand perception) or qualitative (valuable information).

> *Speedy solutions* on the back of searchability. A real strength of the Internet, both in terms of product information and personal preference. Asking Google a question is easy and immediate and results in hundreds of hits on whatever the subject.

> *Specific information* on companies, products or other aspects such as ethical, environmental and political issues. (See the Primark website for an example.)

> *Identity or confirmation* through identifying with a certain product, brand or association with a group of like-minded people (communities). This is manifest in searches for customer reviews, blogs, social media.

> *Freedom of choice,* having the power to come to a decision independently, without the influence of a sales person. The option to return products and delivery guarantees make for low risk. The Internet offers customers this guarantee. If it isn't right, you'll get your money back. No questions asked. No fuss. This is why the Internet has become indispensible to the purchasing process.

Throughout this process, we can identify a number of stages that lead to a decision to buy and via which channel – online or offline.

Delhaize tests the effects of beacons

Delhaize is sending customers of ten supermarkets discount offers when they pass certain products in the aisles. The Belgian food retailer is collaborating with deals app, myShopi and Coca-Cola on this initiative.

Delhaize claims to be the first Belgian retailer to employ beacon technology. The beacons are positioned at certain locations in the store and emit a Bluetooth

---

10 See also Lambin (2008).

signal, which is picked up by the customers' smartphone. Customers do need to have the myShop app installed.

Each beacon has its own unique ID, allowing the app to notify customers of a different deal or cash-back offer. With this trial, customers who walk by a Coca-Cola product will receive an alert. The three parties involved hope to roll-out beacon technology across Belgium.[11]

In the book *Shopping 3.0*[12] then again in *The End of Shops?*,[13] the purchasing process is described in four phases.

The *orientation phase, information phase, communication phase* and *sales phase*. Latest research suggests that a fifth, *after-care phase* can be added here, mainly because after care can contribute significantly to repeat purchase behaviour

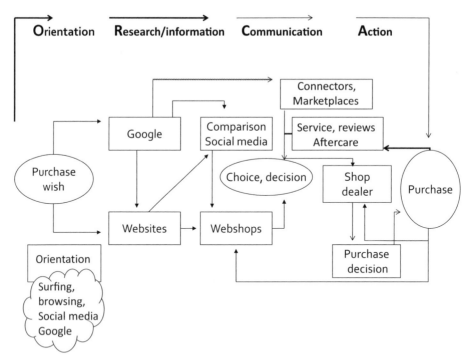

Figure 5.2   Customer journey – after care is part of the buying process

Source: Molenaar (2010).

11 Retailnews.nl (2014a).
12 Molenaar (2010).
13 Molenaar (2011).

(behavioural loyalty), and also because reviews and social media (attitudinal loyalty) can represent a motive to buy. As such, unlike customer support, after care is no longer considered as support for customers who have bought (i.e. falling within the purchasing process), but has come to represent a part of orientation and purchasing motivation (positive and negative).

Orientation Phase

During the orientation phase, there is an impulse to buy. This impulse can be latent or manifest. The difference being that with a manifest impulse, a *need* to buy a given item is felt. The customer expressly searches for a particular item, or deliberately chooses where to buy. Search and orientation behaviour is clearly goal oriented. In addition to this manifest need, there is of course an imperative, or directed requirement. This implies conscious decision. The need might be for foodstuffs – necessary for survival. In this case, buying behaviour is different, and so is the purchasing orientation. A consciously-driven need is controllable and predictable. There is a definite search for a certain item of clothing, brand or product. The orientation phase may take longer because the choice is considered and re-considered. The need is detectable from the way the customer conducts themselves in the shop, or from surf and search behaviour online.

Unconscious orientation is another part of buying behaviour. Visitors to shopping centres nosey around without specific intention; unconsciously, they look with the view to buying. The Internet equivalent is browsing, going from website to website until you are tempted or triggered. It is at this point that the true orientation described above kicks in. In a physical shop, this point may arrive through surprise (a new item) or in the form of a good sales assistant. Smartphones are becoming more significant in the orientation phase because they allow customers to make direct comparisons online. When you've spotted something in a shop, you look on your phone for more info or for comparable products (sometimes via Facebook or another social medium) before you reach your decision.

A manifest need occurs suddenly. It is immediately opportune, partly fortuitous but partly controllable. A need may arise following a certain development: a customer may suddenly be made aware of a risk that needs to be mitigated and take action. Film footage, TV documentaries or news items may trigger such realisations. The first thing the customer then does is visit the Internet and orient themselves towards a purchase. The immediacy of the Internet allows companies to react quickly to these opportunities. Google searches can help direct customers, and companies' own websites can be quickly modified. Direct links can be sent via email or smartphone. This alertness is a prime example of how easy it is to react on the back of customer orientation and how a proactive attitude can in turn drive sales. Popular TV shows have a second 'screen' in the Internet. This second screen provides viewers with additional information and a degree of interaction, as well as opportunities to buy. Asos in the UK and US fully exploits customers' desire to sport the latest fashion in its *ASOS, as seen on screen* offering. Emotional buying is thus stimulated via this supporting second screen. Incidentally, the customer flies through the various buying phases in shopping this way.

This orientation phase is more relevant to items that are bought on a less regular basis. The need to shop around to come to a decision is greater in these cases. During this phase, the decision around buying opportunity and channel of purchase is not a conscious one. As suggested, the phase might begin with a trigger, conscious or manifest. But the role of social media is also growing. Posts on Facebook, Pinterest or Twitter alert you to interesting products, that you subsequently check out online. Social media also has a part to play in the information phase and the sales phase. Experiences had by others and recommendations from friends stimulate to buy. The orientation phase is not necessarily tied in with a particular medium or location. Whilst much Internet browsing takes place in the home, it can take place just as easily in a café, restaurant or simply when passing the time. What we see in orientation is hybrid behaviour: shops, smartphone and computer. Shops are visited and explored and the web is consulted, email and social media are perused. Whilst enjoying a drink on a terrace somewhere, you might be checking your Facebook messages and be triggered by something a friend has posted. Which then spurs you to pay a visit to a shop. Overnight, the smartphone has come to form an integral part of the physical buying process, a hybrid buying process. For retailers, the challenge is knowing how technology – Internet in particular – can be applied to support physical shopping.

The orientation phase is followed by the information phase. Information is sought to back the purchasing decision and can extend to company information, topic information and product information.

Company information is available on the majority of sites under headings such as *What we stand for. Our products and services. Press releases. Contacts.* This generic and functional information can influence the purchase decision. However, this is supplier-led, not customer-led information. Whether or not this is the type of information customers like to hear, is by the by. Companies simply put it out there without asking and listening.

The main purpose of a website like Primark's is to communicate company messaging or strengthen brand image. Retailers have begun to supply much more information around the company itself and the products it is selling.

Product information can be found on individual brand stockist websites which are intended to communicate informative as well as emotional information. Attractive websites and user information often presented in video format are image-focused, but feature next to practical information on products. User manuals, frequently asked questions pages and listed supplier details encourage customers to buy.

Topic information centres around the customer's issue or theme. Information is provided on topics such as health, weight-loss, physiotherapy, how to shoot films, holiday destinations, product comparisons. The theme is leading on these sites, with information being presented in a Q&A format or blogs dedicated to specific sub-themes. Links to websites or individual shops selling a relevant service or product are often integrated. Although these sites are information-led, they clearly guide the purchase process and facilitate sales for the parties involved. Be they a webshop or a physical shop (searchable by postcode).

We are steadily seeing more and more of these 'integrated theme' sites with a blatant commercial goal crop up. Think of tourist information sites on city destinations and city maps that feature shopping information next to tourist information. Or 'connectors' that link straight from one site to a (web)shop site based on information you've provided. Other websites can quickly offer participant retailers a selected target audience, having grouped retailers together in a so-called virtual warehouse. Fashioncheque, for example operates a cheque system, where cheques are bought and can be redeemed at participating shops. The shops are expressly named. In both examples, the offering of online and offline shops is wide. This pooling of information can be useful. Comparison sites such as www.comparethemarket.com compare the products of numerous providers to make buying easier.

Every one of these developments makes for a *more conscious purchasing process*, greater transparency and a better-informed purchase. For this reason, sites of this nature perform a useful linking function between orientation and sales. Mobile Internet is significant too here in its ability to integrate this online and offline search-and-compare behaviour. Location-based information and offers can be applied to guide customers to a stockist at a shopping centre or to relevant search results.

Website information can serve to push a sale on websites with a shop facility, or to reinforce brand image or preference on websites that don't have a shop. Information is no less important to physical shops, however. Whereas at one time, the shop owner was the expert who advised the customer, nowadays the customer knows more about the product than the sales person. The consultancy role of the seller – and with it the role of the shop – has changed. Customers arrive fully informed, loaded with very precise questions regarding a product. If the sales person doesn't have the answers, or needs to read a brochure to do so, customer trust is broken. A far better response would be for the sales person and customer to look for answers together on a terminal or a tablet. That way, the seller is in a position to elaborate on and explain what the customer has just learned. Customers appreciate this and would certainly not frown upon it or mistrust the sales person as a result. Sharing information, openly and honestly, remains key for shops. The challenge is in turning the curious into customers.

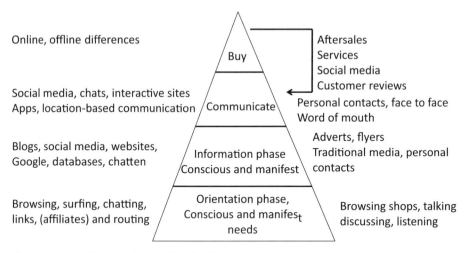

Figure 5.3   Interaction with the Internet during shopping

Communication Phase

Communication is an important part of the buying process and an area webshops excel in. It is used as a means of building loyalty and persuading people to buy. In physical shops, communication is personal. But cost savings, more complex products and increased consumer knowledge have changed things dramatically. A pleasant chat is no longer enough. Customers need to be persuaded with hard facts. Communication during the buying process is centred around the product and its application. Online, it is easy to link up product information and make connections with other products. Support in the form of 'frequently asked questions', videos and email is an integrated solution to communication. These days, the function of communication is becoming increasingly important for webshops. Online videos and animations provide good bases for communications. Social media and peer-to-peer communication is another channel that is gaining ground. In contrast, communication in physical shops is restricted. As a result of cost cuts, staffing is low – both quantitatively and qualitatively speaking. This is a real *negative* for the customer, who is forced to turn to the Internet for the support they need. Whilst they're there, they might as well buy off the site. Shops need to be far more committed to their communications, both in stores and through new media. This might mean tablets for sales staff, as is seen in Apple and Mediamarkt stores, terminals in shops which allow customers to carry out searches to questions themselves, and the application of smartphones. Microsoft and Apple use iBeacons to recognise customers in store, be it face recognition or recognition of another kind, such as by mobile phone number. This information, when paired with the customer's whereabouts in the shop, is then used to send a direct 'push' notification to that customer, with product information, price and any discount offers that apply. This creates direct interaction with the potential buyer. To avoid any irritation on the part of a customer, an 'opt-in' clause can always be used as soon as someone comes through the door; a short message requiring the customer's approval. It is precisely herein – the access to information – that lies the potential of technological development to enhance the value of physical shopping. Examples in practice are QR codes on shelves or products themselves. Just scan the QR code to receive all product-related information on your smartphone or on the shop's computer screen. Rfid chips are another possibility. An item of clothing with an rfid chip attached (they are the size of a grain of sand) is held up to a special mirror which activates the chip's data file, a website or a video. This immediately shows the customer any product information or user instruction.

> At Burberry, customers can pick up a garment that is fitted with an RFID (radio identification) tag and trigger an interactive video that shows how the product was made or what other items complement it.

> Angela Ahrendts, CEO of Burberry, says this gives in-store customers access to the rich levels of immediate information they have grown to

expect from the online experience. "Walking through the doors is just like walking into our web site," she says.[14]

Communicating means wanting to share things with others – be those others other (web) shoppers or friends. We will start seeing more shops with mirrors allowing customers to immediately post the image in the mirror on Facebook or Twitter. The same goes for selfies you can share. The reactions you receive on the back of these posts will help you make your purchasing decision. The Internet facilitates this type of activity, but more facilities for this interactive customer are needed in physical shops, too. Communication is important in the lead up to a purchase, but also afterwards. Compliments from peers are confirmation that you made the right choice of product. Dedicated websites or themed sites that link to Facebook make this possible. But communication is also paramount in fostering customer relationships. The shop you once bought something from sends you email updates; after searching for something online you start seeing more and more banner ads from companies that sell

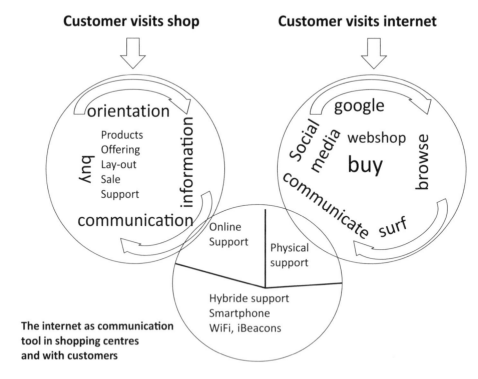

Figure 5.4   Support with the Internet during shopping

---

the thing you were searching for. Communication creates attachment and is persuasive; it also serves to entice. Physical shops should take advantage of this by using customer details to send out direct communications (via the Internet) and to smartphones. The latter is of particular relevance to retailers, as the communication can be rolled out to customers whenever they are the vicinity of the shops. This can be done on an individual shop level, but is far more impactful if done at a collective level, by and for the shopping centre or shopping area. The result is targeted communications without risk of bombarding customers' smartphones with messages. For privacy reasons, it is advisable to offer an 'opt-in' via app. (There is of course also an opt-out option). Future applications of big data will make it possible to send highly targeted, personal messages to customers. Data supplied by the customer, together with historical buying behaviour tell an awful lot about a customer's purchasing intention. Advanced analysis systems facilitate instant reaction to a customer visit and to their buying behaviour. The direct targeting we see online and on webshops should be emulated by physical shops. Why would you go to a shop otherwise? Denying the new buying behaviour, failure to employ new resources and non-collaboration will only lead to problems. *Safeguarding the old through pain and strife is not the way. Customers simply shop differently these days. Customers need new motivation to shop at shops.*

After-care Phase

Historically, after care did not make up part of the purchasing process. The sale had already been completed, and after care was about solving any problems that ensued. This is no longer the case, mainly thanks to social media, and the role of after care has changed. When customers make a nice purchase, they naturally want to share this with the world. Followers and friends see what's been bought, online or offline. The role of after care has become two-fold: to support paying customers and to stimulate potential customers to buy. The purpose of an NPS score, which we came across earlier, is to cultivate ambassadors of a brand, company or product. Highly satisfied customers (scores of eight and above) enjoy boasting about their good judgement. This is the group to target. Existing customers are of influence during the information and communication phases. Social media plays a key role in this, and companies need to be proactive in sending, reacting and observing. *Listen, learn and react.*

But companies can also actively influence buying behaviour through guiding opinion forming. A well-used tactic is to supply bloggers with material. Successful bloggers often boast tens of thousands of followers. By getting the blogger on-side, you can indirectly stimulate followers to buy. Carefully scanning the blogger's Twitter followers for comments can be equally useful in establishing whether the consensus on a product or company is positive or negative. A blogger relationship built on content will encourage positive product/company feedback to his or her followers. Companies should be au fait with who the influencers on customer buying behaviour are. In addition to bloggers and 'the Twitterati', these persons are those who are active on Facebook, celebrities, famous people, advisors and 'middlemen' such as connectors or review sites. The earlier mentioned theme sites are important in the purchasing process, and thus require a clear policy. Market influencers can be divided into three groups:

> *Standard influencers* are those who exist in the physical world. This group includes 'word of mouth', hearsay and recommendation circles: friends, acquaintances, customers, users and colleagues.[15]

> *Advisors*, this group is well represented online, namely because customers making non-food purchases will research the Internet for advice and suggestions on things they don't buy on a regular basis. Advisors are bloggers, review sites, connectors and social media.

> *Companies* can also push sales. Links to social media, customer interaction, reviews, comments. All of the above encourage purchasing. Affiliate marketing, whereby sites are connected with each other, is also significant. Affiliate marketing involves drawing customers in to direct traffic to the affiliate site. For example, in a list of published works, there might be a link to the site selling his books. Similar affiliations can lead a reader from one information-based site to a second site selling reviews or publications. The affiliate site profits from the image and trust the initial site enjoys.

Another modern form of influence is viral marketing. An online ad campaign goes live via social media to attract attention. This might be in the form of a provocative clip that friends and colleagues circulate. On Facebook there are thousands of clips that have been forwarded on or added to people's timelines, which is a great way for a company name to be in the spotlight for positive or negative reasons. Viral marketing can encourage or discourage sales.

---

15 For a detailed description, see Gladwell (2002).

Uploading photos and selfies produces a similar effect. All of this user activity creates what is collectively known as User Generated Content. Users generate content and disseminate it amongst themselves. Companies need to keep a close eye out to be able to anticipate or respond to reactions.

In the end, all the noise has to lead to sales. Everyone has their own preference for on- or offline shopping; the shop as the traditional place of purchase, the Internet for its convenience.

Social Shopping

Shopping is closely tied to hedonism, inspiration and experience. These social needs also present themselves in the build-up to a purchase, in the browsing phase. Recreational shopping, noseying and days out in the centre illustrate this. But people bounce off each other in the virtual world, too. Social media are made for this, which include video sites as well as the well-known friend and network sites. Video is a good way of sharing with others and finding your way online. YouTube is the best known and most used video site. Young people in particular rely on images to identify what it is they want. User-based sites are also well suited to this. Suppliers of smartwatches and sport watches have their own websites via which they share information – such as running and cycling routes – and exchange training tips. These communities deepen the consumer's connection with a product and brand, but also with the subject matter. As such, retailers glean valuable information regarding how their products are used and valued. This can translate into targeted offers or research. This insight can also be put to use during the purchasing process, with product suggestions being offered on the back of historical purchases. A fan site or inspiration site takes this a step further. Customers can 'converse' and help each other find the best product for them. There are many examples around of customer support sites that offer solutions to (common) problems – a prime example of users helping one another get optimum use from products. For Apple, these sites, made by and for Apple customers, are an essential part of technical support and customer service.

International Retailers

Foreign webshops also form part of the choice customers face during the purchasing process. Shopping has extended from local and national to international. Sometimes we are aware that we are dealing with an international firm, but that can also be reassuring in a way. Zalando is opening up the shoe market from a head office in Germany and German warehouses. Amazon.com does the same from Germany and England. In Belgium, most e-commerce sales go to foreign players, the Dutch at the top of the list. As a result, a proportion of Belgian customers' disposable income is spent outside of Belgium – an economic loss for the country.

These international retailers take advantage of the disparate developments across the territories. In Europe, England, France and Germany are the forerunners. The Netherlands is for them a logical new market to target. The same applies for American retailers who surpass their European counterparts. This is aided by the fact that resistance towards American retailers is low. China's retailers face more resistance from other territories, but it may just be a matter of time. As these companies continue to work on their image, privacy codes and product codes (*anti* child labour), they become more interesting to the European customer. The initial public offering of Alibaba, which achieved an incredible $220 billion in market value, is proof that Western investors have faith in the vigour and potential of Chinese webshops. Providers like Tmart. com already have a number of warehouses spread across the various continents to allow fast delivery from that part of the world. This also creates a chance to adapt to the region's specific purchasing preferences. Alibaba has a war chest of $22 billion, which will undoubtedly go towards further development of foreign trade. The Chinese authorities will have no objections. This development will be good for the Chinese economy and significant help develop the countryside. Not to mention the fact that the sons of China's rulers are involved in Alibaba and will share in its success.

Technology and Buying Behaviour

The following chapter will discuss the role technology plays in customers' buying behaviour in detail. We don't need to look into the future to be able to do this. Technology is always present in the purchasing process. TV adverts, customer cards, access security and card transactions are some current examples. Over the last decade, the Internet has also become an integral part of retail and customers' buying behaviour. The application of the Internet can be split as follows:

- Application to support the purchasing process.

- Application to guide buying behaviour.

- Application to influence circumstances.

There are countless developments that support buying behaviour. The buying model outlined here involves the application of technology at every phase:

Orientation phase: the use of rfid chips and interactive mirrors in shops; websites, themed sites and communities online.

Information phase: terminals and mobile apps (based on QR code or rfid chips) in shops; various supplier websites, webshops, technical support online.

Communication phase: iBeacons to follow customers through shops, location-based services with terminals and location-based apps.

Video sites such as YouTube, social media in all forms, question and answers forums and interactive websites.

Buying orientation: automated mobile phone payment function, scanning and multiple sales and discount activities in shops.

Product suggestions, facilitation of purchasing and payment transactions, suggestions and pointers to a variety of popular sites following the purchase.

We will witness many more examples of this application using the smartphone with the arrival of improved identification systems, better analysis systems and better communication systems. Shops need to invest more in technology and show more of an interest in the possibilities they have to offer customers. Passively waiting and playing down the scale of developments is disastrous.

Buying behaviour is steered by triggers such as discounts, others having bought an item or suggestions based on historical buying behaviour. The impact of big data is yet to become far greater in the physical world. The combination of big data, analysis systems and communication systems will allow for instant, real-time analysis of data and communication with customers. This will in turn allow retailers to better respond to physical presence, customer knowledge and customer behaviour. Fast analysis methodologies and the smartphone make instant control possible, as is already the case on the Internet, including instant analysis of browsing and buying behaviours. Given that computer

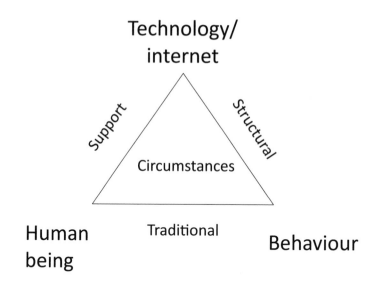

Figure 5.5   Role of the Internet during shopping

capacity is due to increase rapidly over the coming years, we can expect significant developments.

Going, Going … Gone?

If customers are show rooming, walking away from the shops empty-handed and going online to make their purchase, the shop proposition must no longer be meeting the needs of the customer. A different proposition is needed to guarantee shops' continued existence. Customers buy on hedonic grounds. Shops therefore need to take a lead from the catering industry in terms of experience and opening hours. If customers are disputing shop prices, then they are not appreciating the added value in the shop's higher price tag. More work is required on services, experience and benefits to the customer of buying direct. Retailers need to work harder to sell, motivating customers to make purchases. This requirement is something very different to constant price reductions.

The Internet is used heavily by customers throughout the purchasing process. Retailers need to be aware of this and be equally as present throughout the process themselves. A sound strategy includes keeping an eye on social media, for example, customer satisfaction levels and the increasing role that 'after care' contributes to new purchases being made. Customers are buying differently *because they can*. The change in the purchasing process has lead to disruption in retail, affecting everyone involved – directly or indirectly – in the retail model. The system is about to change, with huge consequences for shops, shopping areas, municipalities (property taxes) real estate and suppliers. If, going forward, these parties fail to join forces and adapt to the wishes of future and existing customers, the future of shops as we know them will be in doubt. This need not be a foregone conclusion – so long as parties work collectively! Is it not absurd for a council to think that building a new bypass will encourage customers to shop? Enforcing paid parking when we know that this is a turn-off for the shopper? Is it not enough that increasing vacancy levels are costing money due to less tax being collected? The existing retail model is nearing the end of its life cycle. But it is not unique in this respect. The chapters that follow will elaborate.

PART 2
The World We Get

A world dominated by technology

A world without privacy

A world of continuous communication

Chapter 6

Signs of Disruption

The last few years have seen the introduction of new applications in quick succession: iPad, iPhone, sensor systems, webcams and video control systems, as well as online and mobile payment systems. Each of these has come to take up a permanent place in our day-to-day lives. With the adoption of these innovations, we note changes in the behaviour of consumers and companies alike: firstly, in a more efficient use of existing systems; secondly, as the application becomes more and more accepted, it becomes more and more effective – often new applications based on old structures. Adjusting systems involves a combination of applying new technological solutions, adapting to (predicted) customer behaviour and taking a fresh look at how structures, systems and organisations can be attuned to the technological possibilities of today and tomorrow. This adjustment implicates practically every customer, company and government data system. Customers alter their buying behaviour in no time, so adjustment to this altered behaviour needs to happen just as quickly in order to keep up. That said, adjustments can be complex, and sometimes costly. Existing companies often resist making changes on the financial grounds that they offset profits. Consequently, action is taken too late, after a competitor has already taken over as market leader.

Systems Adjustments

The initial phase of change is not revolutionary. It often involves doing an old thing in a new way. Mobile payment is a new, more effective and efficient form of payment than the traditional PIN code and cash means – the smartphone has made it possible to pay for something straight out of your own account, anywhere in the world – but the form is still traditional. In the same sense that webshops are in essence no more than a shop that happens to be on the web. Despite people now shopping online instead of at the shops, the phenomenon is still classed as shopping. Flight tickets are now printed off as opposed to written out, as they were previously. TV nowadays offers a myriad of channels, but has that altered how TV is watched? Over recent years, we've witnessed all kinds of new applications slot into old behaviours and old structures. We've now reached the tipping point where structures will be adjusted to meet new innovations and solutions. This is the next phase of change that will see the introduction of new possibilities. Systems are based on new solutions, of which the disruption described in the first chapter of this book is an inevitable consequence. Or, in the words of Professor Andrew McAfee: 'We have arrived at the 33rd square on the chess board, with a doubling in computer capacity and application possibilities'. A whole new application of the possibilities (systems and means) is upon us. The basis for this lies in the sequence of innovations that have come about in the last few years. Yet the moment existing systems and structures are adapted, more new innovations appear in quick succession. An example of this is the smartwatch. Originally a new form of timekeeping linked to computer possibilities, the smartwatch soon evolved to become a health monitoring device, sensor system, identifier and responsive tool, via which cloud-like signals could be sent and received by cloud-like applications. This enabled help to be called when required, location to be pinpointed, navigation assistance and anything else you could possibly dream up.

We see the same development in automobiles. How far away are we from driverless cars? Higher-end vehicles are already equipped with navigation systems that respond to the traffic situation and queues, sensor systems that react to the speed of the car in front and offer suggestions as to the most economical speed or driving style. These are the same sensors, responding to external factors that will build the driverless car.

Meanwhile, future users are leaning towards these new possibilities. The fall in new car sales is in large part down to altered buying behaviour. Improved car quality of course means that cars run for longer, which in turn helps demand for second hand cars, but at the same time, having a car no longer features so highly on people's wish lists. Enjoying convenience and facilities no longer means possession, but possibilities. Public transport, taxis, hire and lease cars are all options. Car sharing is another. Further possibilities are being developed through the Internet, such as the online taxi portal, *Uber*. By installing the Uber app on your mobile, you hail the nearest participating taxi to you. This removes the burden of having to speak to a particular taxi firm's call centre (and long waiting times). The result is disruption to the taxi industry and a competition between the old and the new. Banning Uber, as is the case in Germany, is nothing but naïve and no different to banning environmentally unfriendly cars or cars caught speeding. Taxi firms also need to adapt to this new possibility. Why not develop a challenger to Uber? Surely what will follow next – the driverless car – presents a far greater threat to taxis. On activation, the car turns up before you and transports you to your destination of choice. As soon as you've got out, the car sets off en route to the next user. Trips into town are efficient, easy and save on parking. A great way to enjoy all the benefits of a car without having to pay for them. Consider the implications: parking fees and council budgets, car parks, insurance companies, revenue from fines, petrol stations, car washes and the rest of the infrastructure that is built around car ownership. What we are describing is not some sort of utopia. This is already reality. Uber is already operational and fewer cars are being sold and consumers are ready for this change. If car-related expenses fall dramatically, more of the budget can be allocated to other items (health care, pension or leisure activities). The knock-on effects this potential new solution will have on the logistics of delivery vans, unnecessary trips and competing logistics providers will be touched upon later.

Many car-related businesses will of course suffer. Then again, these were precisely the businesses that benefitted from the disruption to transport that was caused by the very introduction of the car 100 years ago. That disruption coincided with changes in consumption expenditure that came with increased prosperity from 1960.

The Uber app as an example disruptor is not new. A similar development has taken place in the hotel industry. Bookings.com (and priceline.com) spotted an opportunity to make life easier for customers looking for hotel and leisure accommodation. It became no longer necessary to call or email individual hotels to check availability before booking. Booking.com essentially did this for you by displaying potential hotels and their availability almost instantly. The site also provided customer reviews and listed room rates. Anyone with a smartphone or computer could now make direct comparisons between hotels, view the rooms, read reviews (expressed in a numerical score), compare prices and book their accommodation. The convenience of the concept appealed to customers, and the success that followed had consequences for the industry. As more and more bookings were being facilitated via booking.com, hotels' own booking systems were starting to become redundant. Customers' booking behaviour led to the reservations department eventually being outsourced.

The issues arose much later. Hotels lost a grip on their own bookings. Booking.com did display room availability, but only of a (often small) percentage of a hotel's rooms. If a hotel showed no availability on booking.com, people would perceive this to mean that the hotel was fully booked and would not pursue the issue with the hotel direct. As a result, hotels were left with low occupancy rates. In the end, booking.com had to disclose its policy on the website.

A second source of irritation was the commissions. Hotels pay a commission to booking.com for their hotel to be listed and bookings to be handled. The percentage of this commission and overall costs of using the facility did not sit well with the hoteliers. Meanwhile, booking.com's market position was so strong that the hotels couldn't afford not to be involved. These are clever tactics from booking.com, of course, but also perhaps a way to put blame on the hotel industry's slow reaction to the possibilities of the Internet and to customers' changing buying behaviour? Is this also not down to lack of vision and collaboration? Most hotel chains used a standard booking system that was tailored to their needs. Booking.com is a generic system that takes bookings for all hotels and helps them attract guests. These guests are fully informed about the available hotels, so that they can make the best choice of hotel for them. The system clearly suits customers and clearly represents disruption in the reservation of hotel rooms. Slow reactions can lead to loss in market share. At best.

The same is true of the world of travel. Flight tickets, trips, cars, holidays and hotels are all booked online. Customers find what they want and prefer to use established online companies, Sunweb being at the top of the list. It is now considered rare for someone to visit a traditional travel agent. Even though not so long ago this would have been the first point of information for any holiday. Still, if customers see no added value in what a travel agency can offer, the motivation to consult one is lost. Far more fun to spend a Saturday night together researching destinations, checking availability, comparing prices and reviews, discussing it with friends on social media and booking a holiday yourself than sitting in a dingy, depressing office. This goes for everything from a flight ticket to a backpacking holiday, tailor-made trip or an all-inclusive. The customer-traveller knows what to look for and is often better informed than agency staff. Many travel agencies have shut down, but tour operators will also struggle if they take too long to react to these changes.

What is in fact happening is that the rigid, supply-led structures are coming under pressure from these new developments. The initial reaction is to optimise the structure, make it more efficient, then subsequently review the structure to assess whether it can be made any more effective. This happens through collaboration, shared warehousing, online order collection depots or working with local points of distribution. But disruption will occur here too, forcing existing parties to adjust if they are to be successful in the future.

Part-timers, staff cuts, less regular postal deliveries and other cost-driven precautions simply won't cut it anymore. Perhaps the whole system needs a shake-up. DHL has already started delivering with Drones and Amazon.com is in the process of a Drones trials, as we saw in Chapter 1. This is the first step towards disruption and there are more to come.

Automation and drone delivery allow customers to specify a precise delivery time, eliminating the painful wait for a delivery and the issue of being out at the time. Dedicated collection points for Internet orders will also become obsolete. The first step towards this is multi-doc applications and city-hubs. Initially, these will help maximise efficiency. They will also come to represent disruption within the logistics system.

Retailers share the same warehousing space so that goods are kept closer to the end user. This allows speedy delivery – not just 'next day', but 'within the hour' delivery where necessary. The drone automatically delivers all packaged items, without the need for human intervention. The multi-doc station is a collective warehouse for retailers. But there's more it can offer. Within the old system, each shop has its own stock. Similar shops in the town might stock exactly the same items, with their associated risks and costs; price and perishability, storage costs, inventory costs and, of course, unpredictability of sales, resulting in excess or shortage of supply. This system is highly inefficient and one that, going forward, will *not* suffice. Webshops, wherever their location in the world, are always cheaper. Plus, if orders can be delivered quickly, where is the benefit of buying from a shop? (This is a rhetorical question, of course based on the discussions in Chapter 1.) Hointer in Seattle has conducted an interesting experiment, integrating technology in the store in order to save on costs and boost service levels. We shall return to this later.

City-hubs are a variation on multi-doc solutions. At a city-hub, shop inventory is held at a nearby location, in the shopping area itself. Suppliers deliver stock to here, which can be transported to the shops within a short time. This permits significantly lower stock levels to be held in the shops themselves, lowering costs thanks to smaller supplies, reduced risk and smaller square footage required. Deliveries from the city-hub go straight to the shop (maybe even by drone) or the consumer's doorstep, on behalf of the local shop. Collection is also an option. The current developments are already leading towards this solution. Not only is the required technology already available, but consumer behaviour has changed following rapid changes in supply. The Primark 'disposable fashion' example clearly illustrates this new buying behaviour. The behavioural shift towards cheaper but good quality items is another indicator. In city-hubs, inventory is a risk that the supplier has to be prepared to take This offers advantages for optimisation and a far better 'feel' for market demand and customers of a given shopping area. But there is one main disadvantage. In the current model, much of the risk sits with the 'channel', that is, wholesaler or retailer. This is nice and comfortable for the producer, who views the shop as its customer. This is why the city-hub solution still meets with resistance. But customers will force this solution through by refusing to shop at shops. Although the Internet would appear 'the baddie' here, it is merely a platform that facilitates new concepts (also in shops). If old structures do not change, then customers will indeed head to the Internet. It is up to suppliers' preparedness to work together with retailers and logistics providers to develop new systems. What is it to be? Will a new structure facilitate consumer behaviour or will existing providers cling onto the old and swallow the consequences?

Structures Adjustments

SHOPS NEED TO ADJUST, BUT SO DO SHOPPING AREAS

A decade of development has created the current offering and concentration of shops. In the preceding decades, customers had no choice but to go to the shops to buy, and only during times dictated by the shops themselves. For decades, municipalities practised a shop-unfriendly policy. Why not? Customers had no alternative, but this is no longer the case. Customers are mobile, selective and have the Internet. What does the future hold for shops in shopping centres and town centres?

Shops and shopping centres need to motivate customers to come and shop. Today, shopping is all about emotion and hedonism. Shopping (at shops) is but an alternative to shopping online. Shopping areas must therefore be appealing, pleasant places to visit, and town centres need to be brought in line with the buying behaviour of the modern customer. Shops, catering facilities and culture are key, and close collaboration is needed to re-establish customers' connection to town centres. What's needed is the illusion of a *dream world*, built through lighting, experience and inspiration. Town centres and shopping areas have an important role to play in this. Customers use the Internet rationally; they go to town for an experience. In future, adjustments to the existing structure will not suffice. Benches and flowerbeds are not a strong enough pull to get visitors to a shopping centre. Technological applications, such as iBeacons, location-based services, apps providing useful information and sensor systems hooked up to lighting concepts, on the other hand, are. The appeal of town centres will lie in the catering options, terraces and small independent and specialist shops that vary from place to place. Perhaps there is no longer a place for all those shops in town centres? New shopping centres could then create a different dynamic to attract customers, like outlet centres. The limitations of town and city centres with historic quarters will attract a different kind of customer; or visitors.

THE TOWN AS THE ORIGIN OF SHOP CONCENTRATIONS: THE FORMATION OF CURRENT STRUCTURES

From 1848, there was a clear distinction between town and country. Towns and cities were recognisable from their gates and walls, newspapers, town physicians and other features such as city guards, auditorium and theatre. It's clear that from early on, towns were a mixture of shops, work, culture and safety as well as a number of care facilities. Towns people were very different to farmers and country folk. The city was 'within' and anything beyond was 'outside'. As today, the town back then was the administrative, economic and cultural seat of the region. Towns still have great influence on work, shopping facilities (economical), culture and care facilities that are available in an area. In this context, we could say that there has been a further concentration of these activities around the towns of today. Thanks to economic growth during the 1960s, more and more shops cropped up on the outskirts of towns, in districts and villages. Recent developments – altered buying behaviour linked to Internet sales – mean that we are once again seeing concentrations in and around towns. With the development of cities in the nineteenth century came an urban drift: urbanisation. New, modern towns and cities rose next to historical ones.

THE BIRTH OF SHOPPING CENTRES

At the end of the nineteenth century, centuries-old historical towns and cities adopted a different position. The new, modern cities relegated the historic city to 'inner city', a commercial centre with an increasing number of shops, office, cafes and restaurants that were taking the place of housing.[1] From 1950, following enormous urban sprawl, these historic centres were reduced to city centres. Residents moved to outer areas, suburbs and dedicated dwellings or districts. These suburbs were actually only intended as residential areas. The better the transport links, the more the suburbs would grow. Shopping, home life and work were no longer integrated, but separate affairs. The car and public transport provided links between these domains. Dormitory towns,

---

1   van der Woud (2012), p. 26.

office parks and shopping areas were the result. Customers needed to make a trip out to the shops in order to buy.

This new town had its own structure and rules. Traditional family connections that acted as a social network became looser. With this, a sense of security was lost, along with unwritten rules and rituals. In their place came formal, legal rule and institutions. Local government was given more and more responsibility, while citizens were given less. Official bodies took over the care obligations of neighbours and families and at the same time spurred individualism. Although this did result in a degree of social security, distrust among the community grew, also in respect of the government.[2] City centres were changing too. Initially the city's commercial centre, with historical buildings having to make way for modern architecture, the town hall included. As a result, the coherence and unity of a place were lost. Economic development would eventually create uniform shopping streets, monopolised by identical retail chains. The residents, the people, were long headed for a commuter town or suburb. The car had become a binding factor.

In its former life, the city was a sensory experience: theatre, small specialist shops, markets, well-lit streets, pubs and lots of people. For the 'out of towners' this was a spectacle that wasn't available where they lived. The city appealed due to the facilities it had to offer, but also due to the sensory stimuli and melting pot of people from all walks of life. The city attracted visitors with its modern outlook, one that was visible, audible and palpable. People enjoyed these modern ways and went on little strolls, window-shopping, got carried away by shiny products, bright lights and the atmosphere. (Even back then, the notion of a dream world rang true.) People watching – with envy or appreciation – was popular, particularly on Saturdays and Sundays. These were the highlight of the week, with the working week over. People dressed up and wanted to have fun and be seen.

The new residential areas were nice to live in, but all identical and much of a muchness. The homogenous estates couldn't have been any different to the heterogeneity of the old city centre.[3] The evolution from historic city, to historic inner city, to the towns and cities we know today is a process that has not only brought change, but also much wrongdoing in its wake. Pawnbrokers, criminals, poverty, pollution and appalling living conditions were reasons for the government to govern the cityscape, regaining order, regulation and

---

2   van der Woud (2012), p. 31.
3   van der Woud (2012), p. 48.

safety. Previously, the people themselves and social structures would have performed these regulatory tasks. Nowadays, more and more is conferred to the local authorities. In turn, the local authorities try to re-regulate and place more onus back on the individual, just like old times. Today's mass scale and huge associated costs ask for a reversion to the structures of old. But people have changed. The duty of care that existed previously is now met with protest. Economic order, whereby income was determined based on level of skill, is now controlled and regulated. Shops that relied on clientele and turnover are now large chains that live by spreadsheets. Still, the characteristics of times gone by are a good guide to the foundations of the modern day. Current developments point towards a reversion to old structures and values, but applied within the context of the present day.

CURRENT DEVELOPMENTS: THE BASIS FOR DISRUPTION

Dwelling is returning to the city centre. Older generations in particular like to be near others and live in the vicinity of culture, theatres and shops. The young look for entertainment and dining facilities – equally good reasons to live in the centre. This is no different to the olden days. Pedestrianising city centres is also proof that the centre is seen as a cluster with its own characteristics and qualities.

Work is coming closer to home, or even done from home. More and more self-employed persons are working from home or a local cafe. This generates new connections and new possibilities.

Families take *joint care* of the children. Emancipation and women's place in the workforce have dispelled traditional gender roles. Men are also doing their bit for childcare, or staying at home and allowing their partner to work. Care of parents is another key consideration. Do we bring them into our homes, have them move somewhere closer to us or put them in a care home? This discussion alone is a sign of adjusting to a new era, or perhaps a hankering for old structures; from deregulation to individual accountability.

SINGLE PERSONS

Over a third of all households are single-person

Private households can be split into single-person and multi-person households. A good third (2.6 million) of all 7.3 million households is single-person (see

Figure 1). The single-person household is the most common type of household. Households consisting of couples with children and couples without children are the most common type of multi-person households. Couples without children and couples with children represent 29% and 28% of total households, respectively. Approximately 10% of multiperson-households are single-parent households, of which 83% headed by women. The average size of a multi-person household is 2.9 persons.[4]

The number of single persons is increasing, not only in the Netherlands but all over the Western world including the UK. This is partly due to an ageing population and increasing life expectancy. But this figure is also growing among the young. University is one factor, as are divorce figures, but so is individualism. The family is no longer considered the cornerstone of society. Single persons have taken over. Numbers of single women are higher than numbers of single men, in part related to the fact that on average, women grow older than men. Single persons have a different buying pattern and other living requirements. City-centre living is ideal, with facilities and nightlife all on the doorstep, and the town's social aspects help combat loneliness.

---

4   nationaalkompas.nl

Chapter 7

The Place of Shops
in the City Centre

City centre shops need to be actively attracting customers. The old values apply once more: the hedonic aspects of the town make shopping fun. Shopping areas thus need to appeal on grounds of atmosphere and a good combination of greenery, technology, recreation and lighting. Opening hours need to coincide with the times customers want to buy. It should be the customer, not the store or the authorities who dictate when. If shopping is becoming more of a recreation, a form of escapism, then it makes sense for shops and catering facilities to be available at the times customers want to buy. As drinking and dining are fundamental to city living, food and drink outlets need to work closely with the shops. The structures and principles that apply to the catering industry, such as hospitality, professional and personal services and opening hours will therefore apply increasingly to shops too. Adjustments to shops in shopping areas need to be made if town and city centres (and shopping areas) are to remain – or become – vibrant. The government has a *duty* to keep city centres well looked after, both from a historical perspective and from the perspective of the city's reputation at large. The shops, culture and catering options that a city has to offer may appeal in their own right, but they also contribute to a shared appeal. Only in this way, by working collectively on the hedonic prospects, will town centres remain appealing as places to shop and live and make a positive contribution to the happiness of the local population. Still, in order for the same town centres to be future-proof, disruption to other systems – along the lines of city-hubs and big data – is also required. Large shops will disappear from the city centre scene. Smaller shops will replace them. Entertainment will become a priority, as will culture. Centres will be smaller, unique and inviting. Franchises and chain stores will retreat to a mall that's situated close to the customer and will fully integrate the opportunities made available on the Internet. This pattern is already underway in some countries. In the UK, a new dynamic surrounds major cities; small specialist shops and good restaurants are making the centre a destination of choice. The

Senses
Greenery
Convinient footpaths
Tidy centre and shops
Sound and light
Dynamic guidance on mobiles

Technology
Geo-fencing
Smart posters
Interaction
Website
Loyality rewards

Services
Online routing
Home delivery
Integrated catering
Collaboration

Shopping centres
A dream world for visitors

Facilities
WiFi with geo-fencing
Links to mobile data
Customer database
Customer and database analyses

Communication
Via database
Via Loyality scheme
Ad hoc and weekly
Via mobile

Management
Centre's management
Foundation
Entrepreneurs

Lock-in, connect, reward, facilitate

Figure 7.1   Attracting customers to shopping centres

big chains are located at dedicated precincts and draw in customers in a very different way.

It will take time for this all to materialise and it is essential that the relevant authorities are proactive, not through prohibition, but through motivation and facilitation of the desired developments.

Big Data as a Basis to Change

So much information is available: about ourselves, our behaviours, desires and (purchase) history. The illusion that any form of privacy still exists is nothing more than an illusion. Cameras observe us on the streets and systems regulate our behaviour online. From payment systems to our mobile phones, our behaviour is recorded and linked together. Even the rubbish in bins can be traced back to a single household to check compliance with the rules. Identification, registration, analysis and interpretation occur on all levels.

This is not necessarily a new phenomenon. Consider the situation in the Eastern Bloc during the Second World War. But it happened closer to home, too. And still does. Computers and computer technology have made it easy to gather, interpret and use data. Initially, the system was a closed one. Each organisation had its own data system – from the government to businesses and associations. Data was recorded manually to begin with, but from 1960, appeared more often on information carriers that could be read by a computer. Since the arrival of the Internet in 1990, it has become increasingly easy to collate information and to link sources of information together. This was further accelerated with increasing reliance upon new machines that formed part of our day-to-day lives – machines in which information also formed the basis. This is as true of all Internet use (identification is a condition to accessing the Internet), as it is of smartphones (which are based around communication but linked to identification) and all payment systems requiring a PIN number, smartphone or bankcard.

Initially, the objective was to find a more efficient way of recording data, reading devices or OCR. Automated responses and processes would evolve from this point in. Companies would use the data to conduct their own analyses. The data was also useful for marketing purposes and used for customer analysis, market research, financial administration or direct mail. But the more information that was collected, the greater the need to assess its quality and integrity. It also became useful to link sources of information together. The late 1980s saw a breakthrough with the introduction of the bar code and EDI for standardised data exchange. Throughout the 1990s, more and more files were linked, partly because it was technically possible and partly because this was proving useful. Effectiveness of the data and data analyses also became important. Data was now being assessed based on its quality. The closed systems – a department of a company – were becoming more and more open, extending to the wider company or even beyond the domain of the company. Every department had its own data structure that needed to be made uniform. It became clear that a collective system was required. Data was pre-structured (per user), but more and more unstructured data appeared thanks to the use of computer systems. Till data, payment data, financial reporting, telephone data and mobile data. These data sources needed to be linked to provide an overview of what data was relevant and what meaning could be ascribed to it. A need for ever-more advanced systems arose, as did the need for supplementary sources. Information is shared increasingly. Amazon.com, Google and Facebook share information with third parties regarding Internet use, their sites, buying behaviour, conversion rates and much more. This acquired data can be combined with own data (data fusion) providing further insight into processes, systems and behaviours. Profiles are constructed on the back of historic behaviour and predictions made on future behaviour. This facilitates better planning (efficiency), communication (effectiveness) and helps shape business models.

Retail has become more and more part of a digital process. Customers are attracted by a direct message that has been devised using advanced algorithms and predictive models based on a combination of previous behaviour, profile data and trend data. Social media are key here also. Thirty-five per cent of all Amazon.com sales are initiated by recommendations given on the basis of these advanced analyses.[1] Customer reviews and messaging on social media are considered to be 10 times more effective than messages from a vendor. According to Mackenzie and others, this isn't all. The distribution system will also change. Same-day delivery will become the norm and loyal customers will enjoy free delivery. All systems will need to dovetail into each other for orders, deliveries and returns.

But the fight for customers is only in its infancy. In addition to the aforementioned distribution differences, retailers will also start trying to sell competitors' profit-making products. The old term for this was branch diversification. Nowadays people speak of concept stores or theme shops. However, it is also possible to benefit from each other's successes. Following in the footsteps of Amazon.com, Bol.com offers a marketplace for other retailers. This provides existing shops with a sales platform and represents 20 per cent of Bol.com turnover (after just four years). Data is also shared (sold). In the future, these online retailers will also have their own marketplace variations that allow customers to sell second-hand products. Bol.com, which enabled second-hand book sales, is an example. To take things a step further, products will also be available for lease. After leasing an item for a given time period, the item will be returned and replaced by another new item. Some telecom companies in the US operate similar lease contracts on mobile (smart) phones. This idea plays to the wants of 'early adopters' who are prepared to pay more than the laggards. As such, the handset can be 'sold' a number of times over.

Globalisation is another development. Natural borders have almost disappeared and retailers increasingly have to keep an eye on foreign competition. To most Internet suppliers, international delivery is no different from domestic. Often customising the language of the website is all that's needed (consider Alibaba's Aliexpress.nl). This represents a huge threat to the West from Asia and results in the need to adapt the retail model (lease instead of

---

1   MacKenzie, Meyer and Noble's (2013) article explains the current issues in retail in great detail and provides an account of what's to come. This article forms the basis of this analysis.

sell, for example), the distribution model (quicker delivery, same-day) in order to retain market position. Bear in mind that large international players keep a stash to one side for takeovers, renewals and for opening up new markets. Alibaba picked up $24 billion via an IPO; Zalando €2 billion. Google, Apple and Amazon all have plentiful war chests to be able to outdo each other and win over new markets.

BIG DATA, ANALYSES AND CUSTOMER KNOWLEDGE

Retailers are feeling the pressure from the competition and altered buying behaviour: pressure on turnover through Internet sales and pressure on margins through stiff competition from within their own market as well as from new entrants, from the Internet and from abroad. Mackenzie suggests focusing on five key aspects:

I   *Increase revenue and margins through diversifying products and services*

Retailers have a lot to gain from this. The existing model still focuses heavily on the transaction: revenue minus costs equals net profit. But this is exactly where the battleground lies, with heavy competition on price. The entire retail model is under strain thanks to greater market transparency and waning customer loyalty.

Amazon.com supplies 35 per cent of all total products sold on its platform via third parties (affiliates, partnerships or producers) or via its marketplace participants. In addition, Amazon also operates as an IT partner. The data that Amazon sells amounts to one billion dollars (net) in turnover alone. It also offers computer capacity through web services, making cloud services available to all those who are interested. This currently accounts for a turnover of $3 billion. It poses the question, is Amazon a retailer, logistics services provider that is temporarily offering a data hold function, or an IT provider? Whatever the case may be, Amazon has broadened its base to make more profit, allowing it to sell products at low prices. Going forward, it is important that retailers do not view the retail model as a logistics model, supply chain or transaction-led model, rather as a model that allows you to offer more products and services on the back of customer loyalty and customer knowledge. *The retailer's base must increase and expand* to ensure future success. Simply selling products via a transaction model is not enough. Close collaboration with suppliers or manufacturers is required to secure continued supply.

2   Plan out how costs can be reduced

The extent of price competition means that costs for retailers must go down. A common initial reaction to the changes in the market is for a retailer to launch a website alongside their shop. This reaction is understandable, but often unsuccessful. How is an independent retailer supposed to compete with the pros? For larger retailers, this isn't a problem. An omni-channel strategy works because the shop already enjoys brand recognition, has a number of stores and also has the financial means to invest in a professional Internet strategy. A small retailer couldn't do this, but there are other options. We have discussed hooking onto large websites like Bol.com, eBay.co.uk or Marktplaats. nl, benefitting from the traffic these sites receive. This would of course involve paying a percentage margin, usually between 8 and 12 per cent, but it is a good way to generate 'cash' for other activities quickly and without risk. These Internet retailers attract a specific group of customers, who would also discover you. Why not sell discounted items via this type of platform and keep the shop a pleasant, discount-free zone?

Another option is to launch a site in collaboration with sector colleagues, like Topshoe.nl did. This pools resources and increases local presence through participating stores. Or join forces with the other shops in the same centre/precinct. The key word here is *collaboration*. It might sound strange, but this constitutes disruption in the retail sector and adaptation of the system. After all, the retail model was based on a product supply chain that ended at the shop. Or as one gentleman put it during the 2014 Shop.org Summit: 'Retailing is about moving goods around the world'. Albeit so, this is not a sustainable model. Shops need to work together with Internet parties, suppliers and with each other and be guided by the customer's purchase intention and motives. Connections between customer/retailer and manufacturer need to be tight. Entrepreneurs need to work together with their local counterparts to keep the shops nice. Without some form of collaboration, the entrepreneur is left to do all these things himself, carrying the burden of the costs associated. But is a shop strong enough alone? Collaboration results in shared costs and increased turnover.

There are of course other options. Tougher deals with suppliers, alternative investment and reward models whereby suppliers take on greater responsibility for inventory. We have seen examples of this in city-hubs and VMI (a method built around the supply chain). Franchising is again another possibility; the franchisee takes over certain functions of the shop, such as inventory, bookkeeping, Internet and marketing functions. The shop's costs fall, allowing for greater flexibility. Franchising also stimulates entrepreneurship more than employment relations, as the franchisee's earnings are dependent on the success of the franchise.

3 Review premises and cost of premises

The cost of premises is significant for retailers. Particularly in light of the fact that in recent years, priority has been given to location. Location was considered to represent *the* principal factor for retailers, notwithstanding the associated costs. Yet revenue per square foot has fallen significantly over the last few years. I use a rule of thumb that says €2,000 in sales for every m^2 is what's required for the average non-food shop in the Netherlands to comfortably break even. This figure will be higher for very popular sites. Even in less desirable locations or small suburban hubs or villages I've come across revenues of €1,300 to 1,400 per m^2. This shows just how tough times are for retailers. Often the only reason some survive is because they have no mortgage outstanding on the property. For rental properties, discussions should be had with landlords without delay regarding the following:

1.   How to increase per m^2 revenue (increase profitability).

2.   Is there flexibility in the rates?

3.   Can a flexible rental model be applied with fixed and variable costs, so that the owner shares in the operating results?

The retailer could also investigate whether it would be possible to generate the same amount of turnover with less space. New technologies such as interactive mirrors, Internet orders placed in the shop or home delivery of out-of-stock items are some innovative examples.

Non-action is *not an option*. Not for the retailers, nor for the real estate players. Last year in the US, 45,000 shops closed their doors. The average new shop is 25 per cent smaller than before. Shopping centres that do not adapt to the demands of the modern consumer will suffer a sharp fall in popularity. In the Netherlands, a great number of towns still have the same shopping centres that were built during the 1970s and 1980s and whose design has hardly been touched. In the US, 15 per cent of these malls shut down between 2013 and 2015 because they were no longer remunerative for the shops, nor for the real estate companies. The Netherlands too is in need of a fresh vision for such centres: adapt or abolish. The disruption in retail and the changes required of retailers to fit the new reality also has an impact on the real estate sector. *Time is ticking for all parties.*

But all the above are still only developments based around existing structures. The changes to stock levels in shops, integration of Internet technology in stores and altered customer buying behaviour (online orders, home delivery and/or collection) will all contribute to reducing the size of premises required. In parallel, shopping areas will also become more concentrated, covering a smaller base. A2, B and C locations will feel the effects, and perhaps fall away altogether. The passive waiting game being played by property owners great and small is foolish. It is essential for them to be proactive and address changes together with retailers and municipalities.

4   Use data and analysis techniques to get to know customers and for more targeted communications

For far too long now, retailers have behaved passively in relation to their customers. A good selection of products and location was all that mattered – the customers would follow automatically. This attitude is typical of a supply-led model. Retailers buy what they think customers will want; suppliers put blind trust in the retailer's instinct. All very much a case of 'finger in the air'. No wonder that now, with so much information and knowledge surrounding buying behaviour being available, this attitude is no longer good enough. Webshops, on the other hand, are proof of just how effective customer insight, appropriate and targeted communication and sound forecasting tools can be. Those retailers who still believe that woolly predictions and experience are a match for the precision of data and analysis systems, will be disappointed. Analysis of customers, customer profiles, browsing and buying behaviour are essential for procurement, timely communication and customer loyalty. These analyses provide detailed information on every customer, every change in customer behaviour and when is the best time to reach out with communications. These are precision instruments, not fingers in the air. Stock can be better managed, changes quickly detected and costs better controlled. Data and analysis form the basis of the new retail system. Making adjustments to the old system will result in further optimisation, but won't result in the level of change that is required, namely knowledge of customer behaviour and foresight into future behaviour. The alternative will result in further discrepancies between stock and non-sales or excess stock. The high incidence of discounting is actually proof that retailers have lost their 'feel' for the market, and that the current instruments of measurement are falling short. Not to mention the financial consequences.

A number of retail chains are trying out new concepts with a view to bridging the gap to Internet sales. Is it possible to interact with customers who visit the shop via mobile phone? This builds knowledge that can be used later on in the purchasing process, but also further down the line to put forward product suggestions. iBeacons that recognise a visitor to a store are an example. It *is* possible to communicate via smartphone. But trials are also being conducted on how the smartphone can be employed to support and guide the purchasing process. Smartphone technology assists customers by displaying product-specific information on their smartphones upon scanning in a product code (QR code or NFC chip). Integrating a link to stock levels is a simple addition to this function. This is what was done as an experiment at Hointer in Seattle, a shop selling leisure wear for men. Men's love of technology was taken as a starting point. The method used here was the same one Amazon uses. Customers are followed, profiles created and purchase suggestions are given both during and following a sale. An example of wording from Amazon is: 'Other customers also bought … '. Hointer is trialling a similar technique in-store.

US retailer Hointer uses robots to deliver your choice of product to the changing room

Located in Seattle, Washington, the Hointer Beta Store is a revolutionary apparel store targeting men. Founder & former Amazon executive, Nadia Shouraboura is banking on the "old" theory that "men don't like to shop." The result is a store that allows men to shop quickly with the help of their smartphone. This newest men's clothing store saves on labor costs associated with shelf replenishment, rather it is powered by robots and the stores' mobile app.

By downloading the Hointer's app on the shopper's android or iPhone, the shopper can try on clothes and place them in a virtual shopping cart. The shopper has a wide selection of apparel to choose from. About 150 styles of jeans from 23 designers are suspended from steel cables within the store. Hointer also sells shirts and belts, each of which has a tag with a QR code.

The most interesting part of this store is that the clothes in your shopping cart arrive in the dressing room within 30 seconds. A specific dressing room number on the app directs the shopper to his clothes. If the clothes don't fit, the shopper can place the clothes in a particular section and request a different pair on their phone. The clothes that don't fit are simultaneously removed from the shoppers' virtual shopping cart. The apparel can be purchased while the shopper is still in the fitting room by swiping a credit/debit card on the tablet kiosk's attached card reader. There is also a similar tablet within the store.

This innovative store format presents a new perspective on integrated retail within a brick and mortar store. Hointer's also tracks real-time shoppers' activity in the store and permits customers to rate the apparel on their smartphone. Hointer's gives brands access to the data on the retailer's portal. With this data, brands can see which pair of jeans, shirts, and belts sell well within the beta store.

Since launch, Hointer has continued to reimagine the shopping experience by adding tailoring of purchases with free, next-day custom alterations. A color-coded system has been introduced to help customers quickly find their category of clothes (such as big & tall, relaxed, classic, or slim fit). Real-time data and user ratings provide instant feedback on which styles are hot and which need to be pulled. Clothing tags are now NFC-enabled, so phones with NFC technology only need a simple swipe to pull up the desired style. Shirts and belts have also been added to the inventory, and magnetic clothes hangers provide a sleek and convenient way to look through the clothes on display.

The founder and CEO of Hointer is Dr. Nadia Shouraboura, former head of Supply Chain and Fulfillment Technologies for Amazon.[2]

Retailers need to realise that only those who adopt a strong customer focus will prevail. Indeed, the only route to achieving this is through knowledge of individual customers, adequately performed analyses that are based on individual customers, and provided there is direct interaction between the Internet and smartphones. Online support during the purchasing opportunity is based on knowledge of the individual and of the customer journey. The same needs to happen in shops, as the Hointer trial demonstrates.

5   Reconsider product offering and variety

In the old retail model, retailers were merely a conduit between the supplier and the customer. Items from the supplier were added to the selection purely on the basis that the retailer thought they would be popular. The shop's strength lay in its location (location principle). The added value in the shop is thus quite limited. Customers need to be motivated to buy from the shop, and customers need to be helped to buy from the shop. This involves more than a straightforward till transaction. Shops need to have extensive knowledge of products, offer more services and provide a degree of novelty for the customer. Technological applications are relevant here: via information screens, smartphone applications or via websites. The offering needs to have a wow

---

2   Retail Innovation (2012).

factor. An example can be taken from Nordstrom in the US. A pop-up stand in the corner of the room allows different companies to temporarily sell their products on a rotating basis. Shops could consider giving webshops a similar opportunity to sell at a pop-up stand like this one. This creates an element of surprise, while increasing footfall thanks to the webshop also drawing customers to the store.

Customer reward is another important aspect. Discounts are trite and seldom lead to long-term loyalty. A cup of coffee offered in a shop is a very traditional gesture, but it is also unnecessary. Although few will decline the offer, it is a rational one without much emotional value. A better idea is to work with local food outlets and set up a free coffee or lunch arrangement to accompany a sale. This creates mutual interest, as well as shifting the link between customer and shop from a rational one to an emotional one. Furthermore, the longer a customer spends in the shopping area, the more they will spend.

There is clearly disruption within retail. Customers expect the same knowledge and service from a local shop as from the Internet. They actually expect more from their local shop. Surely they see them often enough to know them by now? Nothing could be further from the truth. Knowledge is practically non-existent in today's (physical) retail, there are no records of buying behaviour and past purchases, communication rarely takes place at the individual level and use of data and analysis systems is limited. Physical retail is stuck in the *old model* of passing products along a chain and 'adding a bit on'. This equates to no more than moving goods about! This needs to change if shops are to survive. Regardless of how efficient it can be made, the old system is simply too costly because of the number of links involved and its physical basis. This system needs to be adapted – if not, replaced – to become a customer-focused system with integration of technological applications. In effect, one needs to catch the customer in a web, the retailer needs to adjust his earnings model and optimisation needs to be achieved through knowledge.

ALIBABA IS CHANGING THE STRUCTURE OF THE INTERNET

Web retailers in the US are right to be worrying about the impact of Alibaba. It isn't so much the size of the Chinese home market which gives it a strong base, but more about its deviating model. Americans are increasingly convinced that Alibaba is rediscovering the Internet through new applications (in a presentation by Scot Wingo at the 2014 Shop.org summit.) If it succeeds, then US (and European) retailers will lag behind. All that retailers have done so far, in fact, is replicate the old model, online. Many (online) shops simply sell products much in the same way as in the physical shop. Technology now means that customers can be identified during the purchasing process and that the process itself can be recorded. Analysis of customer behaviour permits existing marketing tools to be optimised: Price (behaviour-led); Product (perceived customisation); Place (everywhere); Promotion (direct and behaviour-led).

But is all this really so revolutionary? Is it not still the case that customers need to visit a shop – one that now happens to be online? How do customers manage to find your shop among the 850,000 others? Early tactics involved linking webshops with each other through association, also termed affiliate marketing. Another example of affiliate marketing is the marketplaces mentioned earlier; a number of smaller retailers join up with a popular retailer (such as Amazon.com or Bol.com in the Netherlands) that allows them to benefit from the traffic these bigger retail sites enjoy. Traffic to physical stores is led by passers by being drawn in by an appealing window display. This same model applies on the Internet. It's about making sure visitors are aware of your shop, be it by affiliating yourself with another site or marketplace, or through use of advertising, including banner ads on popular sites. The search for ways to catch the attention of the innocent visitor is fervent. Yet the system remains unchanged. Newsletters are sent to spread 'news' (what constitutes news in this context?), digi-flyers developed as a variation on standard flyers, even traditional media such as newspapers and TV are used to lock in customers via advertising. In short, it can be seen as a repackaging of old systems and old applications.

But the sheer volume of websites and lack of transparency in the offering remain an issue. Hence the popularity of search engines such as Yahoo (outside of Europe) and Google (within Europe) that generate web results based on keyword search. Although this was a forward step in terms of making Internet sites more transparent, it also meant that the search engines became more powerful as they collated more and more information on supply (the websites), demand and on those who stood in the way. Through advanced algorithms, search engines are able to gain increasing insight and make the search process more opaque. Highly innovative technology also affected the transparency of selection criteria: in other words, who knows whether the right sites are displayed? Who determines the order they are listed in? And how do we know that competitor sites aren't excluded? Lastly, there was also frustration around the 'business model'. Whoever was willing to pay the most sat at the top of the search tree, thus also got the most traffic. Furthermore, Google in Europe is almost untouchable. This results in alleged market dominance, leading to the EU wanting to intervene. Clarity is needed on the objectivity of search results and methods. To date, this has remained somewhat shrouded in mystery in the name of competition.

Specialist bureaus dedicated themselves to the possibilities of these search engines and developed tools and knowledge to be able to influence the selection process in a positive way. SEO, search engine optimisation, is a method of website design that increases a site's chances of appearing higher in the search results. Ad words (paid-for) were another topic of focus: what are customers asking and how can ad words help my site get right up there? Through paying for ad words or an advertisement to appear on the search result page, a company is noticed immediately. In no way did the structure of the Internet alter, however. It was still a mass of sites competing for attention. As the Internet was first conceived in the US, the Americans dominate the net. They claimed and won control, not least thanks to the immense popularity webshops enjoy in the US, but also thanks to the sheer size of the American market. The US can be considered the ruler of the world of the Internet. People travel from all four corners of the earth on organised trips to Silicon Valley. Internet companies are visited, start-ups examined. The breeding ground of the Internet represents a source of inspiration to web builders and webshops the world over.

Amazon was the first major webshop to make optimal use of the possibilities the Internet offers.[3] The rest of the world followed, taking a 'copy and paste' approach then making any necessary local adjustments. The only country that took a selective approach to Internet use was China. Foreign websites had to meet very strict criteria in order to operate on the web in China. The most popular foreign sites were shamelessly imitated. What determined whether a site was worth copying was based on its American success. Sina Weibo is a copy Twitter, with over 400 million users and in excess of 150 million messages sent each day. RenRen is a copy of Facebook, with approximately 250 million users, 80 per cent of whom use the mobile version of the site. A social media platform that allows anyone to participate, Douban resembles YouTube in many ways. It boasts at least 100 million active users and 150 million visitors per day. The mobile phone is the new place for social media: Wechat has over 600 million users worldwide. Forty per cent of active Internet users in China make use of this messaging service. Wechat combines a number of possibilities, including live conversation, photo services and messaging. Censorship is of course heavy, but this doesn't stop international use of the service. Over 1,000 employees are busy verifying messages daily, creating a delay in the service.

---

3   An interesting book on how this was done is Stone's (2013b) *Mr Amazon*. Rossman (2014) explores what this meant for the organisation in *The Amazon Way*.

As well as social media of all sorts, there are also many active webshops. Often opaque to the West, these webshops are extremely interesting with regard to China's Internet use and market size. Western companies struggle to operate in China, having to satisfy a myriad of criteria. China also protects its own providers. But another hurdle that has to be overcome is the search engines. Even a company like Zara can't manage it. Zara does not feature among the top 10,000 most visited websites in China. Consequently, Western businesses have to join up with the largest providers in China: Taobao, TMall (part of Alibaba), Aliexpress, JD.com or Tmart.

More online sales in China

Zara is hoping to generate online sales in China through Tmall. Although the company has its own Chinese website, Zara's online success is limited and the website sits outside the top 10,000 most visited websites in the country, whereas Tmail comes seventh. Approximately 100,000 brands are represented on Tmall. According to analysts, more and more Western companies will try to launch in China via Tmall, particularly now that Tmall is asking companies provide proof that they are not producing imitation goods as part of its conditions. Prior to the launch, Zara estimated that China sales would grow by 20 per cent this year. With presence on Tmall, this figure is bound to be higher. Around 8 per cent of Inditex' sales originate from China. Pull & Bear and Bershka, two other Inditex brands, are already present on Tmall.[4]

The rise in the Internet company Alibaba was possible thanks to this shielding of the Chinese market. But this wasn't the only reason. A well-chosen and appealing name, a new concept, connections with numerous suppliers and not least, the tolerance of the Chinese government (sons of the country's leaders occupy management positions within the outfit) also contributed. But so did the fact that Alibaba is more than just a webshop. Alibaba recognised that the strength of the Internet lay in its ability to connect, not to open a shop. Unlike its US and other Western counterparts, Alibaba did not imitate the physical retail structures with all of their limitations as described above. Instead, Alibaba focused on new possibilities and has been growing steadily since 1999. In 2014, Alibaba had over 28,000 employees, net turnover of $7.5 billion and EBIT of 54 per cent.[5] Compare this to Amazon: $75 billion turnover and EBIT of 5.6 per

---

4   Retail Detail (2014).
5   See Wikipedia, 'Alibaba Group'. Available at: http://en.wikipedia.org/wiki/Alibaba_Group [accessed 19 March 2015]. Also, see the Bloomberg.com investors information and company profile. Available at: http://www.bloomberg.com/profiles/companies/BABA:US-alibaba-group-holding-ltd [accessed 19 March 2015].

cent. Alibaba's annual growth percentages are around 50 per cent as opposed to Amazon's 22 per cent.[6] But Alibaba has good profit potential, which leads to a market value of over $200 billion. Amazon has a market value of $157 billion and eBay $71 billion. Alibaba is a combination of Amazon (in terms of selling products) and eBay (in terms of marketplace possibilities and payment service). Alibaba is also taking advantage of the rapid rise in mobile Internet use in China (80 per cent of Chinese connected to the Internet buy through a mobile device.) This represents an excellent growth opportunity thanks to the size of the Chinese market and an advanced mobile platform.

Research shows that for businesses under the Alibaba umbrella, advertising revenue has grown to represent the largest source of income, totalling over 50 per cent of total turnover since 2012, rising to 55.8 per cent in 2013. Alibaba takes second place in the whole of the online advertising sector. Advertising income represents over 60 per cent of revenue. The B2B business contributed 18.2 per cent of revenue in 2013. Despite a decline in this sector, Alibaba remains the leader among KMO B2B e-commerce platform operators. Other sources of income, such as commissions, have shown significant increase in the last few years.

BREAKDOWN OF ALIBABA'S TURNOVER

Table 7.1   How to attract customers to shopping centers

Year	Advertising income	B2B income	Other income
2011	48.2%	35.6%	16.2%
2012	55.2%	22.1%	22.6%
2013	55.8%	18.2%	26.0%

Source: iResearch.com (2014).

THE THREAT FROM ALIBABA

Firstly, Alibaba has a home market with significant growth potential. At present, 618 million of the 1.3 billion Chinese population are online. Half of Internet users actively shop online, 80 per cent of whom do so via their mobile. Secondly, currently, 8 per cent of retail sales are made online. Growth opportunities for mobile use are enormous, and Alibaba is fully prepared to support purchase made on mobiles. Thirdly, these figures

---

6   Digitalbookworld.com (2014).

are impressive. But Alibaba's strength lies in its different approach to the Internet: no more webshops created, but the focus will be on connecting them instead. Customers who log onto an Alibaba site are connected through to suppliers who are connected to the platform from anywhere in the world. The suppliers process the transactions, but Alibaba facilitates. For this service Alibaba asks a commission. Advertising sales represent another significant source of income. Fees to feature high on its search engine results and listings through advertisements resemble elements of the Google business model; commissions on third party sales resemble the Amazon and eBay marketplace models. In addition, there are supporting sites such as Alipay for payments and AliExpress for bulk purchases. AliExpress is actually intended for sales in bulk to businesses. 'Bulk' signifies no more than large quantities of a given product. The minimum order of a product is generally 20 to 50 pieces. This is still possible, but many of the sellers will also sell a single piece. This opens up sales to consumers, too.

Tmall.com is Asia's largest B2C retail platform, allowing companies to sell direct to millions of consumers all over China. A Tmall.com storefront (website) is an essential piece of a leading international company's retail strategy for China, and the most effective route to market penetration.

There are two ways to use the Tmall platform:

• Companies based in China can take advantage of Tmall.com.

• Companies with foreign licences can take advantage of Tmall Global.

Unlike in the traditional model for retail and webshops, Alibaba does not make its profits from transactions. There are no inventory costs, warehousing or logistics costs, or costs from any other aspects of the traditional model. Earnings are from facilitating connections, searching and selecting.

Alibaba wants to connect parties with customers, but also offer all of the necessary facilities so that visitors go from one site to the next when they search, select, pay or send. This will ensure an integrated, seamless customer experience based on trust. The trust aspect is most obvious in Alipay's payment system: the customer pays for their purchase on Alipay using their chosen method of payment (e.g. credit card). Alipay then retains payment until the item has been delivered and the customer is satisfied. Only then does the supplier receive their payment. It is therefore in the supplier's best interests for the product to be satisfactory and avoid any returns. The customer avoids any risk: if they aren't happy, they get their money back. Everything about this model is different to the Internet we know, with its individual websites, shops, facilities and information. There are more differences worth noting, but this integrality is particularly striking. Alibaba has not invested in warehousing, as Amazon has. Nor has it invested in inventory, as webshops do. Instead, Alibaba can focus entirely on fully supporting its customers. The Alibaba model is not altogether new. A number of 'multiside' platforms already exist, connecting buyers and sellers with each other. Sony do it with games and videos; American Express, Paypal and square do the same with payment facilities. This was the beginning of more portal and marketplace applications and what led to today's 'sharing economy', also known as the participation model.[7]

> *Alibaba.com has three important services. The English-language portal, Alibaba.com handles sales between importers and exporters from over 240 countries and regions. [24] The Chinese portal, 1688.com was developed for Chinese domestic business-to-business trade. In addition, Alibaba.com provides a transaction-based retail website, AliExpress. com, whereby smaller buyers can make smaller purchases at wholesale prices. In 2013, 1688.com started a direct channel, which turns over $30 million per day.*

Alibaba's Initial Public Offering was a wake-up call for US providers. Something big was happening, and that something was a giant with its very own structure and own potential. At first, the development was regarded as an opportunity; if Alibaba really was so big, perhaps it was a route into China. American companies began to get very excited at the thought of the potential opportunities for sales. Americans have a certain worldview, in which domination and governance feature highly, but also the view that the US is too big to pick a fight with. Wars happen elsewhere, and the attacks on Pearl Harbour and the WTC of 9/11 came as a shock. The same is happening now with Alibaba. Following the euphoria surrounding the potential of the Chinese market, it finally sunk in that the 22 billion dollars from the IPO might well be used to take a new concept to the West, namely the US, first. This means an end to Internet dominance, a whole new structure far removed from the one we know, long-term vision and very low prices combined with optimal service. During the 2014 shop.org summit in October 2014, every one of the speakers spoke of the threat and uncertainty that this creates. The course of the Internet has been altered.

---

7   See, for example, Westerman, Bonnet and McAfee (2014) for more about business models, specifically Chapter 4 and p. 80.

THE PAYMENT SYSTEM

Banks were historically responsible for payment traffic, first in cash, then by giro. A payment involved either a till payment, or the transfer of money from one account to another. In recent decades, this system has endured a number of modifications, such as payment by cheque – bank or giro – and later, payment by credit card, a concept that came from abroad. The system itself did not change; it was simply a case of adapting the means of payment. Whatever the means, banks were still involved in the process. With the Internet, however, a new trading platform emerged. Initially, this new platform also relied on that same payment system. This changed with the arrival of payment service providers (PsP) and later on through new payment facilities that were provided by third parties. PayPal is an example. PsPs arrange for payment to be made from the customer to the banks. Payment service providers act as the middleman and usually have the contracts in place with the banks, removing the need for webshops to keep entering into the contracts themselves. PayPal incorporated additional services, such as security guarantee and delayed payment to suppliers so as to safeguard the buyer.

Amazon was one of the first retailers to adopt the one-click system using an advanced verification process and by saving banking (credit/debit card) information. This allows orders to be processed instantly, without the customer having to go through a drawn-out payment process. PayPal is an external service that delivers the same benefit.

But Internet purchases and Internet payments differ from the old system. Once again, we see the three stages of disruption at play here. Stages one and two – efficiency and effectiveness – fall under the existing system. Amazon has caused disruption because the processing of payments has become part of the purchasing process. PayPal can also be said to have caused disruption through its service modifications, including delayed payment to suppliers and payment protection for buyers. PayPal can also be used to perform payments between PayPal users and for payments via mobile phone. (PayPal was also developed for payments via a small hand-held computer known as a PDA.)

PayPal offers protection to those who purchase products online through PayPal and do not receive their items or receive the wrong items. The buyer is asked to provide PayPal with proof of despatch so that the cost of the returned product cannot be recovered. This puts the onus on the seller to ensure product and delivery, not on the buyer. In the old system, once something was paid for, it was paid for. Banks took no responsibility for the delivery or items. This has changed thanks to the likes of PayPal and Alipay who have put pressure on the seller. With evidence of purchase, the buyer can get a refund on an item and the seller gets nothing. The burden of proof has come to sit with the seller, completely altering the payment system. In the old system, it was left for the buyer to try and get a refund for non-delivery or wrong delivery of their items.

This protection of the buyer means that sellers need to cover themselves. The most important thing as far as the seller is concerned, is to deliver items bought via PayPal in such a way that they can be tracked and traced. There are buyers who declare non-receipt of a product to PayPal once they realise that the package is not trackable, meaning that its sender will be unable to provide proof of delivery and have to refund the buyer. PayPal was formerly a part of eBay, the auction site. eBay also owns marktplaats.nl in the Netherlands. In the autumn of 2014 it was announced that eBay would be split into two separate companies and PayPal would be launched on the stock market and be able to continue to grow independently. This will allow PayPal to take up a more dominant position within the payment system, on the Internet and in shops. Services can expand further and the company will be in a position to compete with new contenders in the payment services sector such as Alibaba pay and Apple Pay. PayPal will also want to become more integral to payments made in the physical world, in shops, for example. This would provide a single, universal payment method. Rabobank in the Netherlands also launched with this method in 2012 in the form of its *omnikassa*. The method permits payment of any kind, without the retailer having to concern themselves with the collection procedure; this is managed by Rabobank.

The current developments show a new payment system, one in which Internet and mobile payments are significant. What is sought is a seamless link between the customer and the Internet; between the retailer, the machine and the buyer. A further example is Apple Pay, which facilitates payment via mobile phone. A special app allows an online payment to the webshop to be made immediately. The iPhone 6 even has an NFC chip that permits payment in physical shops that have an NFC chip reader or transponder (which most modern, digital tills have). Thus, a straightforward, mobile phone payment system is born. Apple Pay launched in 2014 with the introduction of the iPhone 6. Future applications and possibilities are yet to be defined, but we are certainly witnessing disruption in payment traffic, whereby hardware suppliers and service providers (non-banks) are taking the lead. A form of integration similar to Apple Pay is Alibaba's Alipay: an integrated payment platform for Ailbaba shoppers. As explained earlier, Alibaba connects buyer with sellers and performs an intermediary, facilitating role. Payment via Alipay is kept in a fund until the buyer essentially gives the signal for Alibaba to pass on the money to the seller. This system is very similar to PayPal, with the buyer being protected and the onus on the seller to act in good faith. The future of the payment system most probably lies in applications of this ilk: smartphone payments at tills – via NFC chip or App – processed via third party payment service providers who deal with the banks, credit card companies or any other potential service providers. An integrated solution will be required for online transactions, for the sake of buyer security and easy processing. Examples are Alipay and Amazon. With the spin-off from Paypal, it will be even easier to link these services directly to websites. The main advantage, besides ease of use, is the responsibility that has been conferred on sellers. This grants buyers more security. The role of IDEAL payment will change over time because it represents a traditional means of payment that goes in the favour of the seller. The suggestion made by eBay in 2013 that banks have already lost the race for payment traffic is certainly true for the US. In the Netherlands, this still depends on the future development of IDEAL, which should also look to focus on buyer security, payment traffic aside.

THE LOGISTICS SYSTEM

The origins of the logistics system are in supply. Items were sent from the manufacturer to a central collection point to (e.g. a shop) or an end user (factory or individual). The entire retail system is based on the distribution of items around the world until they land at a collection point (e.g. a shop). Innovations within the systems were based on the advances of technology, which allowed cheaper and more efficient transportation. The system itself did not alter. The whole system – retail and logistics – is a costly one. It is also true that the greatest cost and biggest issues relate to the last mile, in the delivery to the customer, shop or factory. Cost-savings can only go so far, and there comes a moment when the system needs to be re-evaluated with a view to using the solutions available. The role of shops is significant. The need for shops to be made affordable once more has a knock-on effect on this system. City hubs and multidocs that function as an intermediate station for manufacturers and shops are an example of this effect. Stockholding takes place in the supply chain, close to the place of processing or point of sale. Bulk deliveries will be sent on a 'need-to-have' basis in smaller units. This makes new forms of distribution possible, with the 'drone' proving opportune. These local warehouses can also serve as drop-off points for Internet orders, online orders made in shops or as drop-off points for retailers. The main advantage of this is speed and the opportunity for speedy micro-deliveries to retailers. Levels of stock held in shops then fall, as do costs and risk levels. This also resolves the 'last mile' issue.

Other changes to the logistics system will follow from changes to the payment system, whereby items that have been ordered will need to be tracked and traced. (As described in the paragraphs on adjustments to the payment system.) Despatch and delivery will need to be proven in order for the customer's payment to be released. 'Track & Trace' will become an integral part of logistics. The question then arises as to the need for so many logistics providers. Would it not be far more profitable for a limited number of providers to have concessions in specific regions or on certain forms of distribution? With items held at a city hub, a local logistics partner could deliver exclusively in that city's area. This approach would result in high efficiencies, more micro-deliveries to shops, factories and customers, and make time-based delivery easily achievable. Recipients can specify when they want an item delivered or when they wish to collect. This form of concession-based distribution is a variation on the 'hub&spoke' system used in the aviation industry. It involves various companies taking on responsibility for a part of the logistics process. Passengers are in the hands of different companies during different parts of their journey. Doesn't it make sense for the logistics system to be divided into unique nodes? The 'hub' is the central transhipment and the 'spokes' the local or regional partners. Delivery on location becomes possible, and further facilities can be incorporated, such as drone delivery or specified delivery. Local stockholding is also an option, ensuring faster delivery.

The battle in the logistics channel has only just begun. Amazon.com regards fast delivery as an important weapon against its competition. In 2013 the company announced that it would be increasing its investment in warehousing in all of the territories in which it operated. In the UK, for instance, £100 million is being spent on the building of four new warehouses across England. This will allow for same-day delivery, and within-the-hour delivery, where necessary. The battle for logistical hegemony is the battle for service and fast delivery. Local stockholding, the integration of technology, new technological applications and a different allocation of logistical duties will help win that battle.

But technology goes beyond this. The era of distributing items across the globe is reaching its conclusion. More and more assembly and standard production techniques are becoming available, with the potential to alter the logistics system dramatically. Assembly of components close to the place of use is one of these techniques. So is small-scale production. The development of 3D printers is an example. This solution will meet with increasing success in view of a need for cost-reductions as a result of influence from Chinese retailers, and also in light of customer preferences and behaviour. The hub&spoke method can also accommodate production and assembly. Mass production will continue in countries where value can be added (such as Asia), but component parts can also be produced elsewhere. The choice of place depends on which country can offer the optimal conditions. Optimal might mean availability of technical expertise, labour supply or the presence of raw materials or other building blocks. Semi-manufactured goods would then be sent to an assembly site located as close as possible to the end destination. An extra addition of custom-made components produced on a small scale completes the process. Fewer and smaller loads would pass through the logistics channel. Shipment conditions can also be specified per component: specialist or mass; time-led or cost-led.

3D PRINTERS

It is likely that 3D printing will become a part of the logistics system. This will allow for small-scale production at a location close to the user (company or customer). Judging by technological advancements, increases in capacity and costs involved, it is not unthinkable that the central application of 3D printers will first take place in a logistics centre or central warehouse of central assembly site. The printer will also be developed – as was the computer – to be smaller in size, with lower costs and more limited possibilities. In the computer industry, computers used range from large central computers to, mini, micro and handheld computers (a tablet or mobile phone). The whole process and structural development stretched over a 50-year period. The central computers, mainframes, were installed increasingly in a 'hub&spoke' construction. This eventually led to the information and Internet system we know today. Based on these developments, the intelligent 3D printer will also make a breakthrough. This is expected to happen much more quickly, with a handful of variations on the central 3D printer and small-scale printers being introduced within the present decade. This will bring about change in a number of systems: manufacturing, logistics, and – first and foremost – retail.

All existing systems are under pressure and will change at the hands of technology. A new retail landscape will emerge, with a place for webshops, new retailers and shops in the traditional sense. Customer behaviour will dictate how the future looks. Town and city centres will resign from their function as shopping areas, with other shopping sites and the Internet picking up this role. Town and city centres will once more become places to enjoy living in; where catering, culture and boutique shops create atmosphere. These changes need facilitating. Desired behaviours need stimulating (particularly through local authorities) if places are to remain vibrant. We are on the verge of multiple disruptive developments. Making piecemeal adjustments will no longer suffice. What is now needed is re-formulation of systems and processes. As customer behaviour changes, so must shops. Employment of the Internet in all facets is crucial for future success. We still have time to make choices about our future. Denying natural developments, technological possibilities and customer behaviour, while desperately clinging on to the past, is no longer an option.

Checklist for Business Models

- Regularly re-evaluate your business model.

- Regularly recalibrate your business flywheel.

- Look into how to modify your business model before your competition does.

- Regularly re-evaluate your proposition, products and services.

- Investigate whether you can also be a digital brand or develop one.

- Investigate whether you can perhaps collaborate with digital leaders such as Marktplaats.nl or Bol.com.

- Shops will also have to consider selling products through these platforms, at discounts, in order to generate income and to keep shops free from constant price reductions.

- Test and investigate new possibilities as a constant process.

Chapter 8

Communication: The Basis of Customer Relationships[1]

Technology forms an integral part of today's world and certainly the world of tomorrow. The present lays the foundation for the future, with developments showing an evolutionary pattern. Step by step on the way to the future, influenced by opportunities and acceptance from customers and businesses. In this way the future can be steered and controlled. It is essential to investigate the changes and look at the patterns in order to know *what* is happening. But it is even more important to know *why* these things occur so that it is possible to respond to these changes and to have control over the change process. The current changes in the buying behaviour and their consequences show clear patterns and causes that are closely associated with one another. It is not relevant to simply go back to how it was done in the past, defending old structures (such as shopping centres). This would certainly *not* help these shops and shopping centres, because they no longer meet the wishes and requirements of the current and future consumer. But who is this consumer of the future, what do they want and what motivates them? The behaviour and motives of the consumer must form the basis for shops.

The Consumer

The influence of technological developments can be clearly seen in the behaviour of customers. As we have the facilities to quickly gain access to the correct information we are also able to quickly respond to this. A potential information 'overload' is increasingly becoming more of a question of good selection and using the right tools such as a search engine, a social media platform or blogs. These days people are better informed than ever, and can have immediate access to up-to-date information anywhere at any time. This

---

1   For a comprehensive analysis of customer behaviour and customer preferences, please refer to the Digital Shopper Relevancy Research Report 2014 of Cap Gemini (2014).

makes people today more empowered and alert, yet also dependent upon this information. Every message is responded to immediately; speed is important, the interpretation of the information less so. Or, as Professor Yarrow suggests, the need for attention and reputation is greater than ever.

The individualisation has permeated to such an extent that individuals want to have clarity regarding developments, which in their view may not be appropriate. A highly critical consumer is the result, a consumer who asserts his or her rights and who expects more and more from suppliers. Service, quality, the right price, explanation, information and answers to all the questions. In addition, ever greater demands are placed on privacy. This has been prompted by the uncertainty regarding what will happen with all the data (regarding the individual) that is collected. Reports of 'big data' whereby all the details of a customer are known and businesses use this information to carry out extensive analyses, is a reason for concern. But a lack of clarity concerning what happens with that data leads to a mild panic about privacy. Customers find it difficult to weigh up the pros and cons, the benefits and consequences of the registration of this data. Only if benefits can be gained will the objections quickly disappear.

Behaviour of People

Up until the Second World War, and still today in small villages, there was practically no such thing as privacy. This is not such a bad thing, however, because the lack of privacy also has a positive side: cohesion, social control, protection and a close community. Everyone lives according to accepted norms and values; everybody knows his or her place, whereby a uniformity arises, a unity that gives a great sense of trust and security. After the Second World War this uniformity disappeared. The greater mobility of people which made it easier to live and work elsewhere, coupled with the development of mass media, led to a change in these small centres. What's more, in the 1960s there were the social changes, followed by the economic changes of the 1970s (hyper inflation, oil crisis). These changes led to an individualisation and another form of self-awareness. This individualisation initially led to a fragmentation of society into target groups, often based on demographic or socio-demographic characteristics. Target groups of like-minded people, with the same pattern of behaviour were identified and approached by marketing professionals. This individualisation, however, produced an unravelling of social ties and part of the social cohesion that was so typical in most countries of the Western world. The development of large cities, suburbs and residential quarters resulted in a greater individualisation and often to the social isolation as discussed previously. This process has been reinforced even further due to the application of technology.

The 1960s also saw the arrival of mass media, along with the first marketing concepts that came across from America. Sophisticated advertising programmes through the mass media led to new forms of association, and attachment to products and brands. Emerging icons and role models led to changes in behaviour. People began to associate themselves with these modern 'heroes', ranging from film stars to pop stars. Subcultures also arose, which were grouped around a particular attitude to life: age or icon-related. Thanks to these typical behavioural characteristics, marketing professionals were better able to bring their product message across, which led to acceptance of certain products within a target group as a sign of solidarity. Take the jeans example, the type of moped or later a particular brand; people were looking for cohesion and association again.

The age-old certainty that one felt due to the identification with one's parents and the local community has slowly made way for a conscious choice of behaviour and bonding. In this decision process there is uncertainty, which is not only the case during puberty, but also if there is a change in circumstances. Who am I, what should I do and how can I be part of something? Questions that help to bring people security and certainty. This happens by comparing yourself with others, icons or the desired target group. That need for voyeurism is a natural one; looking at how others live, peeping at the neighbours. These days this is all too easy on social media. In addition to this, looking at how others live, think and do things, we can also assess our own behaviour or modify it. But we also have a great need to be seen, a need for attention or perhaps even an increasing degree of narcissism.[2]

We want to show ourselves to our friends and acquaintances; show them what *we* do and what a wonderful life *we* lead. A clear need for attention. We even have as a result the need to attract a group of like-minded people, to make our own target group based on behaviour association or hedonism (emotion). This hedonism leads to a self regulation of the behaviour of people and groups of people. In biology[3] the term 'homoeostasis' refers to processes that are closely attuned to one another which ensure the conditions necessary for life are kept constant. Homoeostasis can relate to various functions of

2   See Yarrow (2014).
3   See http://en.wikipedia.org/wiki/Homeostasis

animals. There is, for example, also the term *'hedonistic homoeostasis'*, which refers to an animal's condition of general well being. As soon as this condition is disrupted the animal will try to restore the balance. Many types of behaviour can be explained by this particular model, such as stereotypical behaviour, fear of separation and various forms of aggression. For humans there is also the fear of being left alone and isolation. And if these types of behaviour can suddenly be explained in this way, then it goes without saying that new solutions will also emerge for cases of undesired forms of behaviour. This could also apply to shopping behaviour. *Clearly the ways in which desired behaviour can be stimulated must be examined.* This is not possible through punishment or prohibition, but can be done through motivation. If shops wish to survive and continue to attract a certain type of people, then customers must also be motivated and desired customer behaviour stimulated. There has to be a balance in the buying behaviour again whereby shops have to once more capture a place in the market. As we read in the first chapter, shops and the non-food market can only remain successful if they focus on these hedonistic aspects. Sometimes animals and people appear more similar to one another than you might initially think.

People have a need for belonging, a need for association, voyeurism and attention. But they also have a need to feel happy, and a need for stimuli and involvement. These are some of the many aspects that determine our behaviour and happiness. In the physical world many of the possibilities for this have disappeared. This has led to a sometimes radical form of individualisation and to an investment of emotions. Professor Kit Yarrow has suggested that these two aspects are also significant with regards to the current behaviour. This radical form of individualisation leads to an often superficial behaviour. Sometimes there is no interest in important matters or merely a fleeting interest and there is actually also a movement contrary to this that wishes deep and significant relationships, both private and commercial. This need for relationships, also significant, can be seen on social media, Facebook in particular. This social medium appeals much more to the need for attention and to be seen. Another social medium, Pinterest, caters for the need to share. As a tool to search for like-minded people, Facebook is *the* platform to build and maintain relationships. Each social medium meets a unique need of the users: Facebook for the tendency towards voyeurism and exhibitionism, Pinterest for the need to share and the need for association based on products and brands, and LinkedIn as a more professional platform where the overriding need is for exposure to companies with a vacancy. All these media replace the old media, from newspaper advertisements to personal contacts. Communities replace the old hobby clubs or card evenings, and the network drinks of old are being replaced by LinkedIn. The old media are too slow and limited for the modern consumer.

Behavioural Change

Professor Yarrow explains this change by suggesting that it is the adoption of technological possibilities that has changed our brain function, which has led to radically different behaviour. For everything that people want these days there is some sort of technological support, which makes today's consumer display a different type of behaviour. This technological support has changed the way we are; we read and search in headings, search terms and short one-liners. We also want to be rewarded immediately with a solution or an answer. We have less and less patience, and waiting is a thing of the past. Five years ago we used to tolerate a waiting time of 10 seconds, three years ago this was seven seconds, but if we now have to wait 3 seconds for an answer or for a website to load then we simply move on. It has to be fast, very fast; patience is no longer part of our vocabulary. This can be seen in behaviour not only on the Internet but also in daily life. Our driving behaviour is becoming increasingly agitated, less tolerant and increasingly more focused upon ourselves. Waiting, driving slowly or being stationary is no longer tolerated in the world of this consumer. Focusing is also a thing of the past. Sitting relaxed in front of the TV watching a programme, reading a book or newspaper seems to be so twentieth century. We focus increasingly less and want to do more and more things at the same time; multitasking is a necessity for the modern consumer in order to belong and survive. The mobile phone has turned us from a subject to an object. Everyone is reachable and controllable. Analyses are carried out on the basis of identified characteristics (people have become numbers so that privacy is not compromised).

People born after 1970 grew up as children in a time when there was always a computer. For those born after 1990 the Internet has always been there for them, and for those born after 1995 a world without mobile telephone, the Internet and computers is inconceivable. Young people live in a different world than the older generation, but even this older generation is starting to be influenced by developing technology, despite the fact that their behaviour is ingrained. But their behaviour, too, is supported by the Internet, newspapers are read en masse on the iPad and the digital TV is certainly not unknown amongst the baby boom generation, those born after the Second World War.

The older generation still want to be provided with explanations, information and plenty of text in order to be able to form an opinion. The younger generation, however, live in the world of highlights, buzz words and headlines. Woolly language or any lack of clarity is not for them. The younger generation want facts expressed in plain terms. They form their own opinions and do not want any help in this. A restless spirit, increasingly more stimuli and a great deal of information leads to stress when having to make choices. But the new technology also has an answer for this; with apps, filters and personal information. Big data analyses all this data before it is presented to the consumer. What used to be done by a company, a journalist or perhaps even a priest is now carried out by the data analyst. Selective information leads to selective choices by both young and old. And this is why people again are searching for like-minded individuals, so that a decision does not have to be made. Simply go along with the flow. Do what your chosen group does. The strength of social media is that the behaviour can be seen and monitored through all sorts of communities. Following the members of the group and mirroring yourself to them determines your own behaviour. In America 36 per cent of sales is influenced by social media. By 2018 this percentage is expected to increase to 52 per cent.[4]

Routine behaviour is also a thing of the past; our brains want to be stimulated, more and more. This is why we see so many different clips on social media. The short messages on Twitter fulfil these wishes with small informative stimuli consisting only of short texts without much detail: belonging, voyeurism and exhibitionism, all at the same time. Shout and you're sure to be heard, and retweeted. Consumers are impatient for new developments, innovative stimuli and new technologies to communicate even better or to have an even stronger sense of belonging.

Our brains have changed as a result, as Professor Kit Yarrow has clearly indicated and which can also be seen in our own environment, even in ourselves. This rewiring of our brain is still ongoing. It has by no means reached an equilibrium, but does lead to other patterns and changes in behaviour. Companies will have to take this buying behaviour into account otherwise communication will go nowhere, customers will no longer go to shops and the effect of old advertising forms will wear off.

Apart from the fact that we think differently as a result of this rewiring of our brains, it also leads to a different type of behaviour. Ingrained behaviour

---

4   Green (2014).

is supported by technology (such as with the older generation), whereas new behaviour is determined by technology such as with the Y generation (born between 1978 and 2000).[5] But on top of this, the effects go much further. We wish to prove ourselves, to show ourselves, we want to be taken seriously. Young people want to be famous, noticed and important. Authenticity is considered important; being yourself, an individual, not a group animal that simply follows. Young people see this too little in their environment, it is all so predictable, so transparent! And this also has an effect on shopping and shops. Shopping streets that do not grab one's attention, with similar shops in every street, are so 1990s. Shops and shopping areas have to be innovative; they have to surprise and encourage bonding. Isolation is now greater than ever before. And this leads to another type of behaviour, as well as another sort of shopping behaviour. The hedonistic requirements that shops and shopping centres have to meet have already been extensively examined: the inspiration, the experience, the ability to surprise and encourage bonding. The individual consumer demands this as a response to solitude and his own individualism. But everything has two sides. With the physical behaviour those human traits of wanting to stand out and be seen come back. We talk about the wonderful shops that we have found, the unique and unusual products or the super discounts that we managed to negotiate. 'A game without losers'. Whether this is true remains to be seen in most cases, but for the moment you are the centre of interest, and that feels good. Discounts of course stimulate this feeling of having outmanoeuvred a prey, of seeing off the salesperson. But shopping is not really about discounts (that's what the Internet is for), but much more about the right products and the enjoyment of using them. Prices are quickly forgotten, whereas irritations last much longer.

As a last major change, Professor Yarrow describes the emotions, feelings that become ever stronger. The more technology there is, the more we wish to feel distinct, and the stronger our emotions. We live on an emotional rollercoaster ride, fed by uncertainty, individualism and a lack of guidance and instruction. Online shopping is a joy; it is so clear and structured, and allows suppliers and prices of products to be easily compared. This provides stability once more, without uncertainty. If you are not satisfied with the product, simply send it back. We need structure and balance in our lives again. Physical shopping is emotion, whereas online shopping is structure and rationality. Together they have a chance in the future, provided they are integrated. But consumers today

---

5   Yarrow and O'Donnell (2009).

Table 8.1   **Different attitude of generations**

Babyboomers	Generation X	Generation Y
Born 1946-1964	Born 1965-1979	Born 1976-1994
Idealistic	Pragmatic, cynical	Optimistic, realistic
Community oriented	Individualistic	Own creativity, individualistic
Living by the rules	Reject the rules	Rewrite the rules
TV	PC	Internet
Limited technology focus	Use technology	Technology is a given
Job focussed	Multi tasking	Hybride
Diversity as consequence of actions	Diversity is a base	Diversity as required
Buying is serious, physical preference	Buying multi-channel, pragmatic	Buy impulsive, direct, prefer online

Source: Based on Jeanne Meister (2008), 2020workplace.com

particularly want to communicate, to have their opinions heard and to belong. Social media are ideal platforms for this.

Based on this behaviour companies continue to develop new Internet and IT applications that will support and encourage the behaviour. These innovations provide a catalyst for the changes: Facebook provides a communication platform, Google ensures there is transparency and bonding, whereas Microsoft supports the buying process and interaction. Apple is the supplier of new devices, a human interface to all possibilities. It is the customer's behaviour and the customer's wishes that lead to the speedy innovation of applications based on Internet technology.

Facebook as a Communication Platform

The strength of social media is the bonding factor. You search for friends and acquaintances based on a bonding element. This element can, of course, be friends from the real world, but also a hobby, an interest, a brand or a shop with which you would like to be associated. But this also means that you are affiliated with various groups and wish to communicate in different ways, even through different platforms. Mobile telephone, computer, various social networks and websites, and perhaps even in different ways such as real-time. It is therefore totally inadequate to just look at how social media is used now, or what impact social media has on our buying behaviour at the moment. It's much more important to look at the developments ongoing in this area; after all, Facebook is still a young company with a great deal of money.

Facebook has already more than one billion users, and why should this growth not continue? How would Facebook have developed if it had several billion users, let's say 70 per cent of the world's population? We can already see that Facebook has a growing income from advertisers (an increase of 65 per cent in one year). Facebook wishes to be the market leader in the app economy. What's more, it wishes to integrate apps in a coherent platform for social interaction. This is therefore a subsequent movement of concentration of suppliers: the combination between parties with the connector in the middle who earns money through connecting and advertising (a similar model is employed by Alibaba). In early January 2014, Mark Zuckerberg gave a business update in which he set out his vision:[6]

- There is a three-year strategy for achieving new types of experiences based on sharing experiences, visions and messages including, of course, videos. In fact an improvement of what is already possible now.

- There is also a five-year strategy focused on solving problems for users who wish to have answers to their questions. A great deal of research has been carried out into this, regarding the possible search methods and information supply used, even the application of artificial intelligence. This is an example of efficiency and responding to the wishes of customers.

- In 10 years' time all applications will have to be channelled into an integrated communication platform. Apps will have to be linked so that you do not need countless apps in order to do what you want.

What will be the effects of this disruptive strategy? Zuckerberg is clear about that, too. Within three years the revenue per user will rise dramatically due to personalised messages relevant to the user. This will create a greater involvement and interaction with the users. As these profits come from advertising it makes sense that increasingly more interesting niches and applications are sought. Sophisticated analysis systems and location-based services support this approach. As a result, the local shop will be visible again, not only the large chains or the major brands. While shopping you will be able

---

6   Farber (2014).

to receive highly specific messages from the local shop or a tip from someone in your network.

In order to achieve this, Facebook will no longer focus on its own, monopolistic app, but will endeavour to have an integrated mobile application in order to realise an even deeper relationship with its visitors while at the same time blocking off its competition. There is already so much to share, such as text, videos, links, photos, locations, events, games and various applications. These all say a little bit more about us and what we want to be. These are only the daily updates; however, it also leads to knowledge in the long term about people's preferences. That is why these applications and networks are linked to Facebook users, so that a sort of artificial world can be created with Facebook at the centre. Its own search engine, Graph search, is part of this platform. But despite the fact that this will soon be launched, many years will still be spent on improving it. Graph search is a crucial part of the 'connected' strategy.[7]

Facebook's growth strategy will not only concern the Western world, the intended target group comprises two thirds of the world's population. In order to bind this large group together a separate approach is necessary for Third World countries as part of the 10-year strategy. The 10-year plan of Facebook is ambitious:

- Provide highly personal, targeted advertisements in newsfeeds that will help to produce higher increases in profit margins and the average revenue per user.

- Produce standalone apps as important spokes that provide unique experiences and are in line with the massive Facebook data hub (the hub&spoke system as described earlier).

- Surpass the traditional search engines with Search Graph which uses a variety of artificial intelligence services.

- Bring the Internet, as well as the increasingly cheaper and more functional devices and data centres to the entire planet, resulting in a flat world and bringing the possibility of joining Facebook to more people.

---

7   *Fast Company* (2014), p. 58.

Ten years is a long time in Silicon Valley, but Zuckerberg says the company is ready to compete at a 'large scale, with ambition and resources'. Those three words – 'scale', 'resources', with 'ambition' in the middle – are an indication of the strategic advantage of Facebook at the moment. The impact can be large thanks to the knowledge and interaction with all visitors, the combination with 'location-based' technology and the use of all other available resources. Facebook is aiming for hegemony on the social network and can therefore be a threat to Google. The recent acquisitions already show that Zuckerberg is serious. There was the acquisition of WhatsApp on 19 February 2014, Oculus VR on 31 March 2014 and the acquisition of a drone company at the end of the first quarter of 2014. Three totally different companies: communication (WhatsApp), virtual reality (Oculus) and a drone business. All different, but they fit in with Zuckerberg's ambition to become the leading communication platform with supplementary services. Communication is clearly the flywheel for Facebook. After all, people need communication to build relationships and they use Facebook as a platform.

Alongside Facebook there are many other companies aiming to achieve dominance in their own domain through such a platform. Amazon and Alibaba both want to achieve such dominance in the retail sector. Where Amazon focuses on low prices and speedy deliveries, Alibaba's focus is more on bonding and creating a solid base. We have also seen the development of supporting payment services that facilitate integral applications of marketplaces and collaborations. Google is also aiming for a similar dominance. Google is associated with a search engine, which makes the Internet transparent. Further developments of the search engine are focused on semantic searches, whereby it is no longer the question that is central but rather the thought behind the question. Intelligent search methods are also used, whereby the expected question is central. As a result, an answer to the expected personal question can be given even before the question is even asked. A combination of Google with suppliers, webshops or platforms is a logical development.[8]

Google for Transparency and Bonding

Google is developing not only on the basis of the search engine, but also on the basis of the transparency it is striving towards. Through analyses Google is able to build up a great deal of knowledge of the wishes and expectations of customers. What's more, it has opted for an innovative form of organisation

---

8   Vise and Malseed (2005); Schmidt and Rosenberg (2014).

where small teams of no more than 10 people carry out research and try to come up with new applications. It is only at a later stage that similar teams come together. In this way, the organisation is able to create a great innovative impulse. Google's ambition is to make the world transparent and more pleasant for everyone. Many projects are aimed at transparency whereby the Internet plays a direct role, through the desktop, mobile phone or other devices. As a result, the impact of Google is not limited to online support, but in particular is aimed at supporting with online facilities. Google Maps, Google Express, Google Glass and experiments with the Google Car are examples of this strategy. In addition, there are new developments on the Internet: Google Search is becoming increasingly more intelligent, Google Shopping connects shops and products whereby it will be able to take over the comparison role, and Google Analytics provides detailed information on the Internet traffic of a website. With all these developments Google is clearly leading the way in its field, and forms a threat to the traditional suppliers of these particular functions. These developments, however, can also provide support for these traditional suppliers who may wish to follow the changes brought about by Google. Google provides a platform that it constantly develops based on innovation and intelligence. In order to make this platform successful other parties not only can and must join, but they will also benefit from the possibilities offered. *Google Express*, for example, delivers orders within one hour to the home through collaborating with local shops, and *Google Shopping* shows products based on the knowledge of customers (for example through the search engine) whereby stimuli for buying are activated. Also, linking searched products on a website and displaying them repeatedly on the search pages of Google is an example of this.

A challenge that Google sees in the coming period is what is referred to as combinational innovation whereby innovations arise through a process of combination. The components of this combination consist of information, connectivity and computing.[9] So much has already been developed that for innovation it is exactly this combination that is important. There is a worldwide information platform, with a possible worldwide approach and practically unlimited computer capacity, for example, through web services. By making the combination ever more specific for a particular market, a new innovative solution can always be offered on the basis of standard components. This can be described as disruptive as the application for a particular business sector changes based on the typical characteristics of this business sector. For the entertainment industry this is different to, for example, marketing or

---

9   Schmidt and Rosenberg (2014), p. 74.

retail. These 'disruptive' applications usually start simply through a small application, to resolve a limited problem.[10] Within retail this was the webshop, which enabled customers to shop at home. In addition to knowing what you are doing (scope), there must also be an immediate focus on 'scale', or rapid growth. This leads to the major winners of the Internet era: the (new) major companies which call the shots and the many smaller ones which will either be forced to follow or disappear.

Google's strategy[11] also followed this path. First, a search engine was developed, with which everyone wanted to work, including Netscape, Yahoo and AOL. Whilst all these companies were busy improving their services, Google not only developed an advanced search engine but it also wanted more. The search engine was already regarded as an open platform, to which other parties could join. The philosophy was that even though this would be at the expense of control, it would promote greater scale and innovation. And Google upholds this principle still today: open, transparent and honest so that everyone can join in further increasing Google's success. It's actually a bit like an oil slick spreading, or the development of a new ecosystem; the Android operating system is a good example of this. As discussed earlier, a flywheel is necessary in order to grow. Google used the search engine as the flywheel for further growth. And the search engine is still the big money maker for Google. Investment in growth goes very well with the wonderful earnings before interest and tax (EBIT).

The flywheel of Google is the connection: the role as *connector*, based on transparency, bonding people and companies.

Microsoft for Sale Support and Interaction

Another important party in the area of computing and the Internet is Microsoft. The research departments of Microsoft, Google and Apple work closely together. Each has its own domain and strategy. Perhaps Apple and Microsoft are each other's biggest competition, or does this just seem that way? Apple works on the basis of a closed domain based on Apple equipment, whilst Microsoft runs on its own operating system. The two companies' histories are also different. Apple comes from the computer world and from the very start

---

10 Schmidt and Rosenberg (2014), p. 77.
11 Based in part on discussions with managers at Google in September 2013 in Mountain View, CA.

has made computers based on its own operating system. From the beginning Microsoft was always *the* operating system of computers with MSDos and later on Windows. From this foundation the differences are clear to see, and the interests in various areas are different too. Microsoft wishes to acquire a dominant position in the mobile market and in the retail sector with interaction (iBeacons and interactive mirrors).

As a late entrant it was no longer an option, but a necessity, for Microsoft to acquire an interest in a company that was already a major player in the mobile phone world. This player was to be Nokia, which had completely missed the boat when it came to the smartphone market. Nokia is a classic example of how an introverted focus on processes and efficiency can lead to a misjudgement of developments in the market. Microsoft's interest of course lies in creating an integral platform based on the Windows operating system (their flywheel), both on personal computers and mobile devices. This standard will enable devices and information to be easily linked, and so help to lead to new innovations. This is very much in line with Google's philosophy of scope and scale, which, as a worldwide application, is important. What's more, a large portion of Microsoft's revenue has always come from its platform (operating system).

New applications are based on this integration. The announced Windows 10 platform is an operating system for both computers and mobile applications. The application of 'OneDrive', Microsoft's cloud solution, makes it possible to store and use data independent of the computer being used. What's more, the combination of gaming and computer use forms a good source of information on user behaviour and motivation. This knowledge can be used for user interfaces and the development of new applications. The beacons of Microsoft are based on Kinect, an application that comes from the gaming world. This makes it possible to identify customers in the shop (through face recognition) and to gain information on the walking, waiting and buying behaviour of customers in the shop. This information can then be combined with the information that the shop already has of the same behaviour of this customer on the Internet. Direct communication, interactive, through a smartphone is then just a small step. Integration based on knowledge and behaviour determines the customer bonding. This vision of Microsoft is based on these sorts of applications in the retail sector. The customer journey is the guiding principle here. It's about customer experience, social involvement and social bonding, as well as advanced analyses and, of course, efficiency in the execution (operation efficiency).[12]

---

12 Based on talks with a manager at Microsoft in Redmond, WA, September 2014.

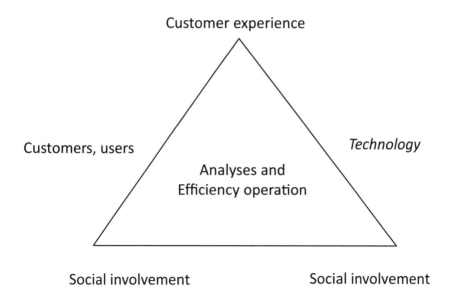

Figure 8.1   **Microsoft's strategy, a bridge between technological possibilities and customer support**

This leads to new applications in the shop such as the combination between retail shop sales and Internet sales, particularly Internet sales in the shop supported by the link with stocks at the logistics service provider (city-hub) or at the supplier. There are digital displays, which allow other products to be shown as well, either as video or as photos or in combination with products that the customer for example displays or carries. This is already leading to all forms of augmented reality, whereby layering technology allows products to be shown over the image in the mirror. By standing in front of the mirror customers can see the collection that is projected onto their own reflection. The clothing can then be tried on without even having to physically wear it. Through the integral link with the Internet and a warehouse, the products do not even have to be in stock in the shop. The articles can be collected later from the shop or delivered to the home.

A tablet can also be used as a means for completing the sales transaction (cash desk), so that the same salesperson can complete the customer journey. Based on the recorded buying behaviour and the products that are viewed both online and in the shop, analyses can be made on the expected buying behaviour. This expectation forms a basis for direct communication, also via the smartphone. This communication can be carried out through email or alerts during an online session or as the customer approaches or is inside the shop.

It is Microsoft's ambition to change and improve the expectations of customers, irrespective of the channel used. Hybrid channels and hybrid behaviour of customers require an integral application.

The old retail model was based simply on sending goods throughout the world. This supply chain would ensure the goods got to the shops where customers could purchase them. This is an expensive and inefficient model as I have already described previously. The innovative application of technology and the integrated technology platform will change this model, enable it to fit in better with the wishes of customers and will become much more efficient. The lower prices and the fast change in the products offered (through the analysis of customer behaviour and customer preferences) will form the basis of this new retail model. The customer will shop when and where he or she wishes, and it is up to the retailer to respond to this. Microsoft's foundation lies in the seamless connection between systems, between 'touchpoints' and customer interaction. The flywheel of Microsoft is the *operating system*, which enables seamless connections between applications (hardware and software). The flywheel for Apple is, for example, the *ecosystem*. This is why Apple is not only a hardware supplier, but also facilitates connections between its hardware and software within its own domain. Based on the various 'flywheels' collaboration in the field of research is possible, with each party making its own contribution to a solution. But central to this is people's behaviour; what do we want, what do we do and what motivates us. The study carried out by Kit Yarrow clearly shows the wishes of the modern consumer.

Internet of Things

As a result of all these developments, the application of the Internet will change; from connecting people to connecting 'things'. Examples of this are the 'track&trace' applications which allow you to follow a package thanks to the scanning that is carried out at transfer points or because an (active) chip has been added. This allows customers to monitor their orders from China or America across the world, so that they know precisely when the order will be delivered. At Alibaba this has even become an integral part of the service, as the payment is finalised only once delivery has been made. Customers authorise the purchase only once this has been received in accordance with the order that had been placed. Verification of the delivery can be done through such a 'track&trace' facility. The burden of proof regarding the delivery therefore no longer lies with the customer but with the supplier. But in other areas, too, such monitoring systems are already active. Through an active RFID chip, people or goods can be monitored live, by means of an NFC chip (this chip is used, for example, for paying without cash). But this technology also makes many more other applications possible. If products are fitted with such a chip, information regarding the product can be supplied immediately, as is done with the application of the shop Hointer as already described. As a result, the customer can choose a product without the intervention of the salesperson. But a chip in the packaging can also lead to innovative concepts, for example in the packaging of foodstuffs and a reader integrated within a fridge making it possible to register the stocks inside the fridge or the foodstuffs consumed (if they are not put back in the fridge). By having the chip communicate and carry out activities, totally new developments can emerge. The Internet is no longer the domain of people, but of connections, also between various products or between products and people. A self-driving car equipped with sensors and controlled through Internet data is one example. There is also the development of a smart home which Google is currently working on that makes new applications possible. The microwave, thermostats and lighting that can be controlled remotely are the first examples of this. But if these applications are integrated and become part of new concepts, then is the following example from Google also achievable?

> *All articles in the fridge or kitchen are fitted with a chip. As soon as the article has been used up a message is sent to a shopping list. At a set time, let's say each week, this shopping list is forwarded to the warehouse of a company selling foodstuffs where robots collect the articles (this is currently done mainly by hand). The articles are then put into boxes and via automated conveyor belts loaded fully automatically into a car. The car with driver, but this can also be a drone, delivers the box to the customer at the desired time. The entire process can be carried out without any human intervention. All the basic household provisions can be delivered in the most efficient manner. As no human efforts are required, for neither the collection nor the logistics, this can be carried out highly efficiently (cheaply). The application possibilities are already available. What we have to wait for is further acceptance, modifications to the structures and a willingness to invest.*

The development of the 'Internet of things' is only in its infancy. Chips have to go further down in price. It is already possible to spray a chip onto a product so that costs can be reduced further. As soon as the cost level drops to below one cent nothing will stand in the way of its large-scale use. In addition, efforts are being focused on miniaturisation – the chip is currently the size of a grain of sand – and on further improving capacity. The 'Internet of things' is the next step in the development and application of the Internet.

The developments described above, of connections, ecostructures and marketplaces, clearly show the pattern for the future. The 'Internet of things' forms the basis of efficient applications that not only provide more services but also lead to lower costs. In order to realise this, the application of the Internet must expand even further with facilities that allow accessibility everywhere and at all times, for people, applications and for the registration of movements (such as with the 'Internet of things' and tracking and tracing). Location data, the identification of objects and subjects and analyses of data linked to triggers and alerts are part of this. Big data, a multitude of data sources, has to lead to knowledge and action. So much is already being registered now, and more will be registered in the future, that the need for interpretation will become ever greater. Sophisticated analysis systems are part of this entire network in order to make the application possible in the daily practice of the retail trade. All these developments really only arise due to customers accepting the new possibilities. This fits in with the 'rewired' consumer of the future. Knowledge of today's consumer and his or her behaviour is essential in order to develop the right applications.

Knowledge and Communication

Knowledge is obtained through the application of analysis systems based on vast databases. Data is translated into information, patterns are identified and this knowledge is translated into actions, on, if necessary, an individual level. This is quite a challenge in itself. The question here, of course, is what the relevance is of this for the retail sector and what this knowledge regarding individuals will contribute. This multitude of data can be converted into knowledge, which forms the basis for strategy and communication, whilst new service suppliers provide the facilities to carry out analysis. It can be compared with Google analytics which provide you with information regarding website visits, where visitors come from and how long they stay. In this way, there is increasingly more information to collect regarding visitors to a shopping area (via beacons and data from mobile phone providers), and regarding the visitors and their looking and buying behaviour in the shops. Service providers can carry out this sort of analysis, even in real time.

Furthermore, there will be concepts that actually bind shops through Internet-based concepts. Google Express and eBay now are the first to provide a link between buyers and sellers (shops). These parties are ideally suited to collect and analyse data, indeed they already have access to many opportunities in the form of a service or advertising contract. The same patterns are possible whereby an intermediary supplies services and adds something extra. Alibaba is based on this link, but is actually a new platform that binds webshops regardless of where they are in the world. The link between shops goes through a connector such as eBay and Google and proceeds at product level. The product is supplied by the local retailer who has the stocks and can guarantee speedy delivery. This helps to create new concepts between the Internet and physical shops, the hybrid concepts that are no longer restricted to large shopping chains but are in fact suitable for small shops. Chain stores such as Macy's and Aurora have similar concepts integrated in their own particular way. In theory the online orders are handled through the local shop, whereby a speedy delivery is possible, although the customer can also pick up the goods from the shop; the customer can choose. What's more, the fact that the transaction is handled locally ensures that there is no discussion regarding who is responsible, the shop or the Internet. This discussion usually arises if there is a question of turnover-related bonuses. The entire turnover is now directly allocated to the shop which then simply includes this turnover for the bonus. It is a pragmatic solution for the company's own organisation structure coupled to providing benefits for the customer, for example, always being kept up-to-date on the process and being involved in the delivery (collection or delivery to the house).

The Makeable World

The makeable world involves making a choice about the application of new possibilities. By having knowledge of the developments, the buying behaviour of customers and the specific characteristics of these customers, choices can be made based on an understanding of the technological possibilities. The retail sector looks too much at the past when deciding upon changes. When shops find themselves no longer being successful they change their interior, the cash desk is relocated or the product range is modified. However relevant these changes may be, they simply remain modifications for changing the efficiency or effectiveness of the shop. Now that customers buy in a totally different manner, this will not lead to a solution for improving the economic foundation or for improving the profitability of the shop. The application of technology, however, can do this, provided it is based on buying patterns and buying behaviour. The retail sector has to become acquainted with the customer and know what motivates him or her. In her research, Kit

Yarrow clearly shows that we have changed. Less focus and an increasing need for stimuli: more and increasingly intense. There is also the need to belong, to maintain our individuality and our need for communication. All new applications should be based on this. Simply setting up a webshop as an answer to Internet sales is naive. This means that you have to fight on two fronts; against the competition in shops on the one hand and against the competition on the Internet on the other. In actual fact this is a hopeless battle. What you need to do is to facilitate and motivate the customer at the moment of purchase or, even better, during his customer journey. This requires making a clear choice. The shop can be very attractive if the total service package appeals to the hedonistic customer. This is a question of motivation and goodwill. A good website can support this.

A further development can involve the application of new techniques in the shop. Paying by means of a tablet or mobile telephone, for example. Other examples include providing support in the sales pitch by means of up-to-date information from the Internet or databases, iBeacons to monitor customers and interactive mirrors to display the entire product range. Direct communication is essential throughout the shop based on knowledge of the customer (profile information) and direct communication regarding the products you are offering. Today's customers are impatient and driven by the moment. Waiting is no longer an option. The split between rationality and emotion is an important choice criterion. The costs of shops have to remain low in order to stay competitive in the future. This competition will be based not only on price, but on the total concept. A modification to the proposition requires knowledge of the customer, direct communication and experience. And an Internet proposition is also essential for most shops; so a presence on the Internet must be integrated to the concept.

In the future, shop stocks will have to be kept small (lower costs per m^2 of floor space and lower risk stocks), but on the Internet stocks can be unrestricted (with speedy deliveries or delivery next day). Customers do not always want to take their purchases home with them immediately. The idea that customers would always want to take the goods home with them arose because shops started to sell mass products. The retailer may find it quite convenient this way, but that is not to say that it cannot be done differently or that customers have another preference. With a fresh look at what can really be done on the basis of technology and the Internet and what customers truly want, new concepts will arise, as we have already seen with Google Express and Alibaba. Change based on an economic foundation (shops) and customer preference is only possible through the integration of new possibilities and abandoning old preferences and assumptions. The world is changing, as is the customer, but this world is also makeable. A condition for this, however, is that a lot more knowledge is gained about the behaviour and wishes of customers. Only then can shops and shopping centres be modified and become attractive once again.

Chapter 9
The Challenge for Shops and Shopping Centres

Customers are changing, and the impact of the Internet on our behaviour is becoming ever clearer. The challenge lies in identifying these changes as described in the previous chapter. The changes are being stimulated by technological changes, but they also have to be facilitated by, for example, shops, shopping centres and city councils. If nothing is done customers will no longer see the necessity of going to the shops. It is therefore important to have a new look at the future of shops, shopping centres and the retail model.

How can the retail sector still make money if customers have ever-higher demands, the competition becomes increasingly intense and if fashion and trends change ever faster? This is an enormous challenge of course, but also a sign that the business world is changing. The traditional transaction model of sales minus purchasing equalling gross profits, and gross profit minus costs equalling net profit, was a simple one. The focus is on making money as well: drive up turnover and reduce costs and you have an increase in profit. Price discounts have always been successful. Lower prices increased the number of sales. All retailers had to do was sit back and wait for the customers to come in. The customers always came from the local area, so the retail policy was fairly simple. Look at what shops there are, what the needs are and then you can figure out what type of shops are needed in the area. But it is no longer that simple. The Internet, different customer preferences and other shop formulas show a clear need for change.

Changes in the Retail Model

The retail model is under attack from new suppliers with another strategy, whereby short-term profit is not the aim. An example of this is Zalando, which has seized the market share from existing suppliers through aggressive promotions. A new concept, a returns guarantee and speedy service at low prices, have all changed the business model of shoe sellers. Media Markt also had an aggressive price strategy, which helped it become the market leader in the Netherlands. Recently, Media Markt switched to a hybrid retail model by promoting the webshop alongside the shop, and integrating the Internet within the physical shops. Amazon.com employs a similar strategy, based on a long-term vision to break open markets with low prices, optimal service and a great deal of knowledge of customers' buying behaviour.

Holding on to the old model with physical shops, inflexible opening times and simply waiting for customers, who have to take their purchases home with them, is naive. More is required to remain successful in the future.

So why do shops still remain popular? Fewer shops are needed; perhaps even shops in other locations, but the bottom line is that customers still enjoy shopping. Shop locations that were established on the basis of past knowledge will not necessarily be successful centres in the future. As we have already seen, hedonistic aspects such as convenience, inspiration and experience are important, and shops, too, have to be part of a pleasant shopping area. Customers go to the fun and pleasant shopping areas to enjoy themselves; bars and restaurants play an important role in this. It is the combination of pleasant (daytime) bars and restaurants and shops that make an area appealing. But feeling, seeing, trying out and advice also play a role. And there is also that important element of instant gratification. You want something, you see it, you become rapacious and so you buy it straightaway. The retailer of the future has to focus on all these aspects. The business model must incorporate the immediate reward, either through a surprising range of products and services, pleasant experiences in the shop or simply an extra reward. Loyalty is a form of this which I will examine later.

The strategy of a retailer's total business concept has to focus on six aspects:

- The *range* must be appealing and combined with interactive support through a tablet or augmented reality. 'No, we don't, I'm sorry' is not an issue, rather it is all about offering a deep and broad range which is possible through integration with the Internet (the long tail principle).

- The *convenience* of shopping; being able to see, feel and take home the products. But the local shop, which you can easily pop along to, is also important. It is about the combination with other shops whereby you would visit an area rather than a solitary shop. A place without shops can be lifeless.

- *Experience and inspiration* are important. The distinction between rational and hedonistic purchases plays a distinctive role in the buying process. It is not the range that has to be central, but rather the demands and, even more specifically, the buying process. The shop has to be part of this. Inspiration and social contacts are important preconditions for a successful shopping area.

- *Solution oriented*. The support offered by an expert in the field can be very pleasant with difficult choices such as when buying clothes or domestic appliances. Reliable and sound advice leads to trust, and trust leads to sales. Replacing good staff with cheaper staff is truly the *wrong* option. It may lead to lower costs in the short term, but in the long term it will also result in fewer customers and less turnover.

- *The feeling* of gaining an advantage. It is part of human nature for customers to want to have the feeling that they have come out on top with a purchase. This can be the case through a discount or a lower price, a gift or something special. Treating or surprising the customers will put them in a good mood!

- *Instant gratification*. Provide an unexpected, immediate treat at the shop, such as a perfumery giving away free samples or a shoe shop providing a complementary pair of socks with the purchase of a pair of shoes. I will take a closer look at the effect of loyalty systems later.

These are six basic principles for motivating customers to go to shops.[1] Webshops were initially seen as the main competition of shops, but this is not really the case. It is actually another type of buying behaviour that leads to different purchase flows. And shops fit in less well with these purchase flows than they used to. People now make their purchases at other times (in the evenings and at weekends) and in other places (outlet centres, fun and pleasant town centres and the Internet). The place of shops in the future will have to be carefully examined once again, along with what advantages shops can offer. This is a challenge for marketing.

---

1   Niemeier, Zocchi and Catena (2013), pp. 116ff.

Threats to Existing Shops

Table 9.1   Threats to existing shops explanation: Existing shops have to compete on a different way

Webshops	A different buying process. Different buying times. Service driven.	Mobile applications (smartphone), consolidation between suppliers. International developments (such as Alibaba). New market victors (low prices).
Low price concepts	New trends such as disposable fashion (Primark), batch sales (Action and other discount stores), low cost propositions (Lidl).	Subject to consumer trends. Dependent on budget choices. Popular due to pressure on discretionary income Dependent on low costs and efficiency.
New concepts	Integration with technology (Hointer), new concepts (Booking.com, Uber.com). New locations (outlet centres).	Pleasant shopping centres with extended opening hours and free parking. Many chain stores and low prices. Various bars, restaurants and entertainment.
Technology	Hybrid concepts whereby the benefits of the Internet are combined (long tail). New services such as home deliveries, active and aggressive communication via smartphone, customer recognition systems and personal offers.	New shop concepts on the basis of hybrids. 3D printing and other supplies. Imploding supply chain and another role for manufacturers. Different financial models and another role for banks.
Customer behaviour	New customer behaviour and customer preferences through changes in social demographics and the impact of technology. Different customer preferences and recreation activities. Less loyalty, more individualisation.	Fickle behaviour, adoption of new technology, other choices for expenditure: more on technology and holidays. Less need for possessions, more for flexibility. Dealing with uncertainties. New generations with different behaviour due to the impact of new technologies. Different way of bonding, restless and self-interested.

MARKETING INSTRUMENTS

Marketing is traditionally focused on products and markets. Bringing products and services 'to market' requires knowledge of target groups, of how to reach these and of products that meet the wishes of this target group. The 4Ps (price, product, place and promotion) are the most commonly used marketing instruments, and are also used in retail. Retail has added a fifth important instrument, namely personnel. These days, however, these instruments no longer work so effectively. This is due both to customers who are motivated to shop in a different way and to technology that makes increasingly more product variations possible for ever smaller target groups.

Price

The price incentive has been exhausted by the Internet and by the possibility of producing goods at very low costs (in Asia), as a result of which further price reductions are practically impossible. Low-price suppliers in particular have reached optimum levels of cost reductions and are satisfied with a small margin in exchange for very large volumes. And it is this volume that is important for the total profit. As soon as the volume reduces, profits will come under pressure. The consequence is a change in concept, higher prices or a termination of the shop formula. It is important to maintain low prices and to realise high volumes, but this requires aggressive advertising campaigns or other high profile activities. Low prices can also be part of a penetration strategy in order to capture new markets, such as that of Zalando and Media Markt. As soon as a desired market position is achieved, the strategy can be modified. This can be done by modifying the advertising strategy, increasing the services or, for example, by modifying the Internet strategy (Media Markt). It is also possible to increase the product range on the basis of the generated customer data, thereby increasing the revenue and profit per customer (Zalando). The current marketing instruments fit in well with the supply-oriented strategy, whereby the supplier determines the conditions of the supply, the opening times, the product range, the price and services. This always worked well as long as customers had a limited choice in what was being sold (only local shops) and if customers had a limited knowledge of the market. *Those days, however, are gone.*

Media-Saturn sets his sights on online pure players

Electronics firm Media-Saturn is going to take over, launch and bundle online pure players into a new subsidiary. To this end the parent company of Media Markt and Saturn has set up Electronics Online Group (EOG), it was announced on Wednesday. The aim of the new subsidiary is to give the online growth of the firm a boost with Redcoon as the main player. This webshop was acquired in 2012 by Media-Saturn. On 1 November Martin Sinner will be appointed as CEO of Redcoon and will also be responsible for the execution of the pure online strategy of Media-Saturn.

'In addition to the online activities of Media Markt and Saturn we wish to present ourselves on the market for online pure players', explains the Dutch CEO Pieter Haas. He sees great opportunities for growth through Redcoon, acquisitions of other webshops and new online concepts.[2]

These days there is little opportunity for physical retailers to use the price weapon. Things are always cheaper on the Internet or at a discount shop. The current mania of constantly working with discounts can be understood in terms of short-term promotions but makes little sense when looked at in a long-term context. These short-term price promotions are simply that, short term. It is important to take into account that certain planned purchases will inevitably take place or will take place as the need arises (latent needs). As a result, price promotions lead to cannibalisation of the current and future turnover, which can be detrimental to the image of the product or shop. These days extra care is required as customers first look on the Internet before making a choice (even by using their mobile phone while shopping). Price reductions would lead to even more pressure on margins. And yet there is a good reason why shops should sell at lower prices now and again. Customers like to be pleasantly surprised, to feel that they have managed to get a good deal. Short-term price discounts can help in this. The need for stimuli, as indicated by Kit Yarrow, can be a reason for attractive price discounts. It should, however, be pointed out that the stimuli need to be ever more frequent and intense in order to have an impact. The sales signs in shopping streets advertising a 70 per cent discount do not lead to busier shops, so I believe something else is required.

A great deal of money is invested in stocks. This money first has to be released before new stocks can be bought. This can lead to frequent discounts, even during the busy months of November and December 2014. Excess stocks lead to the invested capital being tied up, which means less can be invested in a new collection or innovating the product range. And if the product range doesn't change, the shop becomes less attractive to customers. Price reductions benefit both shop and customers. They help to release this capital, which can then be used for further investments to make the shop more appealing to the customers. Sometimes marktplaats.nl or the Bol.com marketplace is used for this. As a result, the shop is able to retain a vibrant feel for customers because it does not constantly have to have clearance sales. The excess stock is then sold at a discount through the Internet. This is a tried and tested strategy particularly in America, but also on eBay.com. Mark downs and clearance sales do not

---

2   Retailnews.nl (2014b).

create a good atmosphere in the shop. In this way, the shopping experience within the shop is not adversely affected. Sales through the Internet can help to not only create more pleasant shops, but also enable money to be quickly released that can then be used for a new collection. This interplay between the Internet (marketplaces) and shops must form the basis for responding more quickly to the buying behaviour of customers.

Place

Shops will change, both in terms of what they sell and where they are located. As indicated in the book *The End of Shops?*[3] there will be a decreased demand for shops and even no demand at all for certain shops. Electrical goods shops have practically disappeared from city centres, as well as record shops and bookshops which have either disappeared or are languishing. There are only a few travel agents on the High Street. The influence of the Internet and digitalisation can clearly be seen. Nonphysical products can be sold more easily and better through the Internet. What's more, there is so much information available on websites and blogs that customers no longer require the help of a sales assistant in the shop. Shops are no match for the Internet, apart from a few exceptions. Other shops have to realise that shopping has now become a choice.

The whole physical shopping area plays an important role in attracting customers and visitors; the entirety of what is on offer, whether it be fun and diverse, whether it has good accessibility, the type of bars and restaurants and the layout of the public spaces. Together they should stimulate the senses and provide a good atmosphere. The success of a shop is determined to a great extent by these environmental factors.[4] Certain outlet centres owe their success largely to the experience they provide, their range and the inspiration they provide. What's more, shops have to adapt to the environment and the type of customers that the shopping centre attracts. There is usually a particular crowd puller in every shopping centre. Account will have to be taken here of the difference in rational and emotional (utilising and hedonistic) shopping. If a supermarket is the crowd puller in the shopping centre then customers will come mainly for their daily shopping.

Steven Jobs (Apple) employed three important principles in his shops:

---

3 Molenaar (2011).
4 See http://www.fedoraoutlier.com/5-leading-principles-of-why--apple-stores-sell-more/

Examine the experiences of visitors, focus on what people do with your product and allow people to walk in and have a look without being approached straightaway. These important principles now apply more than ever to every shop; only by doing this can you support the behaviour of customers.

In the future different shopping areas will exist side-by-side, and will attract different customers due to their own particular look and feel. The city centres will be considered attractive because of their combination of entertainment, bars and restaurants, culture and shops. Shopping centres are very much focused on the combination of shops and facilities for getting people to stay. Attracting people remains a challenge. There have to be constant innovations with regard to experience and inspiration. In the Netherlands there are still far too many shopping centres that have lost their appeal due to a lack of investment in innovation and technological applications. Many shopping centres therefore still look as they did in the 1970s and 1980s and this is no longer attractive for customers. Another development is those centres that do indeed focus on the experience of customers and provide a combination of entertainment, convenience and 'greed'. These outlet centres take advantage of that human instinct for wanting to gain an advantage: that hunter's instinct, recreational activity and stimuli. Currently, constant stimuli and surprises are important in motivating customers to buy. Outlet centres have to do their very best to attract customers as they are often located out of town such as in Roermond and Bataviastad outside of Lelystad. As a result, they actively focus on inspiration. Existing shopping centres are often too passive and simply sit back and wait for something to happen. Shopping centre proprietors simply leave it to the shops to attract customers. This will lead to fewer customers in the future. Eleven good footballers do not necessarily make one good team. It is therefore incomprehensible that for decades city councils have done their best to chase customers away from their city centres due to poor air quality, the environment, lorries and the like. They have enforced high parking costs and restrictive regulations and made minimal investments in, for example, good lighting, access roads, public greenery and other hedonistic aspects, but now complain that not enough customers visit the shopping centres. That's surely what they wanted; customers realised this and so looked elsewhere. Not allowing new shops outside an area and not investing in the old shopping centre is simply incomprehensible. There is nothing wrong with enforcing policy, but there should also be a policy regarding investing in the inner cities so that those areas can be made attractive for living, working and shopping. Then it is much easier to accept the arrangement of 'out-of-town' centres.

Promotion

Advertising campaigns have always been product based, from sender to recipient. Today's customer is becoming less interested in advertising, unless it is personal and directed at a particular need. Advertising has to be based on knowledge of the customer and must be relevant for the individual. Traditional direct marketing techniques such as registering address details, buying information and customer profiles have become a basic precondition. Analysis systems and Big Data applications provide a better insight into customer behaviour and lead to more knowledge regarding the customer. This forms a basis for communication in each phase of the customer journey, right up to the moment of the purchase, and is optimally applied on the Internet. In addition, a customer's attention is drawn to special offers, similar products and the buying behaviour of other buyers within the profile. There needs to be constant communication and stimulation, before, during and after a purchase, but shops actually do very poorly in this. They do not know their customers, have no address details, no purchasing information and absolutely no profile data to identify their future purchase intentions. Retailers simply wait until a buyer comes into their shop. With a bit of luck the salesperson will recognise the customer, but even this is often expecting too much.

When it comes to communication, physical shops are no match for the Internet. It is easy to complain about it, but action is much better. For example, ensure there is good personal communication. This leads to more visitors and better bonding with customers. The wait-and-see approach leads to a loss of customers; a continuous drop in customer numbers in the shop is disastrous for turnover. Technology can help in this, from a database with customer information (CRM system) to direct communication by email. Also, in the future, increasingly more beacons will be used to identify customers. Smaller shops dismiss these straightaway in view of the costs, but do not come up with any alternatives. This is too easy. A customer database for registering the email addresses and the purchases costs hardly anything, but offers many possibilities for personal analyses and personal communication.

In addition to this direct communication, other forms of communication may be possible. Just think of joint communication from a shopping centre, through a centre manager, or via social media. In actual fact, the basic principles of the past should be employed within a new concept.

- You communicate at times that are convenient to the customer.

- You communicate on the basis of a clear message that appeals to the customer.

- You communicate with a clear goal.

- And lastly: the numbers tell the tale: check whether it strikes a chord. If so, carry on and perhaps even intensify it. If not, modify the communication.

Product

As we have seen, the product concept will change. The customer no longer wants to buy a mere physical product (rational/functional) but rather wants the total product experience, image, association and the concept. Personal motives are important aspects here, such as the image of the brand, the presales and after sales service, the fashion aspect and the services. Customers buy a total package of values, physical as well as imaginary ones. It is important for products to have particular added value. In shops this can be personal care, advice and product presentation. On the Internet this may include: service, information and user information. For customers it is much more to do with the usefulness and the association with the product. This has to be clearly indicated. Shops that are little more than a servicing hatch or checkout, and simply a process in which the customer has to look for the appropriate products himself, make no use of the opportunities to add value and so will as a result lose the battle with other purchasing possibilities.

Personnel

The marketing instrument that is the most effective in setting retailers apart from the rest is personnel. How is it that personnel abroad seem to be so active and involved in the pre sales and often also in the after sales? In contrast, in the Netherlands we see savings on personnel costs across the board, whereby services and advice, which are important motives for going to a shop, are being lost. Perhaps that's the reason why a retail job is not so highly regarded? Also, the pay system with fixed wages doesn't really stimulate people to focus their attention on selling. In other parts of the world, with the United States being the best example, it is those variable remuneration elements that inspire personnel to take a more active role in the purchasing (and selling). This can even reach the extreme where sellers have their own shop within a larger shop. A department or part of the department is his domain and the remuneration largely depends on personal results. We also see this form of organisation employed in restaurants where the waiter or waitress is responsible for a number of tables, their shop in effect. The earnings here are the result of their independent enterprise. This form of remuneration does not fit in with the Dutch social model. But a more variable remuneration system would help to stimulate personnel to be more active and certainly respond more to the wishes and needs of the customer. A great deal of turnover (profit) is lost unnecessarily and customers are put off if personnel do not do this.

From the Product Thinking to Customer Thinking

If the existing marketing instruments lose value, other marketing instruments will have to replace them. These marketing instruments will no longer be based on products, but on customers and customer experience.

Table 9.2   Different focus in different markets

Starting point	Existing market	New market
Existing product	Increase turnover	Acquire market share
New product	Sales to existing channels	Sales via other channels

From product thinking to customer thinking

Starting point	Existing customers	New customers
Existing product	Share of wallet	Total concept
New product	Customisation and association	Individual needs

The customer was actually not part of the old marketing model. Only in direct marketing was this the case, because direct communication with your customer is only possible if you have their address and contact details. Since the application of IT, particularly after the 1970s, the use of direct communication increased considerably. This direct communication was later linked to sophisticated analysis systems which provided much more information on the individual reactions and responses. It led to a greater knowledge of the medium, the activity and customer behaviour. The advertising world rather looked down upon this form of advertising; it was considered 'below the line', whereas of course the real work was carried out 'above the line'. Carrying out research, developing campaigns, creating slick ads particularly for television – now, that was proper work! Another aspect was of course the measurability of the activities. This was scary. Advertising was also dismissed as unmeasurable at any activity level. The measurability was determined based on the market shares. Half the money spent on advertising is wasted; the trouble is we don't know which half, is a saying you often hear.

Direct marketing, or rather direct communication, was measurable and as a result the return could be easily determined. The principles of direct marketing can still be seen in direct communication and the Internet. Also on the Internet it is possible to communicate personally in all sorts of ways, via email, newsletters or digiflyers. Direct communication is also possible on the basis of customer behaviour through links with other websites. How long do we seem to be followed by product advertising after looking at a particular product on a webshop? This eventually leads to the final move towards a purchase (50 per cent). Analysis systems are becoming ever more sophisticated, such as big data analyses in which the focus is on the individual customer. It is thanks to the technological developments, with the Internet as the most important flywheel, that the focus can be placed on the customer. This requires a transition in the marketing strategy and marketing activities as well as a change in the marketing instruments. The *Harvard Business Review* of July 2014 had an article on this.[5] The customer was the guiding principle. Organisations have to:

- Carry out more analyses: big data, deep insights and analyses of customers and customer behaviour.

- Have a clear value proposition for customers (purposeful positioning).

- Therefore ensure the customers are motivated to buy.

- Ensure there is a total experience, both of products, shops, aftercare as well as the packaging.

- Ensure there are links with other products, services, suppliers and internal departments (connecting), inspiration and focus.

Collaboration at every level, both internal and external, is essential in order to be able to respond to the wishes of the customers, to respond quickly to changes in demand and to also be innovative (agility). The conclusion that can be drawn is that successful businesses must have a great deal of knowledge of customers and customer behaviour. These companies must think in terms of cross functionality, have a customer focus and be able to quickly respond

---

5   Ferrazzi (2014).

to changes. New organisation structures can support these changes.[6] All these principles are applicable to every organisation, large or small, that are focused on consumers and other companies (in the supply chain).

But most of the organisations in the retail as well as in the supply chain do not have this knowledge nor do they take any initiatives to build up this information. It is therefore not unusual if customers then no longer want to buy or continue buying particular products. If you don't want to get to know me, why should I get to know you? Or phrased differently:

> *A customer allows the shop or product into his life, so why don't suppliers allow the customer into their lives? Sometimes you can compare this with the animal kingdom. The loyalty of the dog is unprecedented. But the reason is clear. A dog fits in with the life of the owner, and the owner in turn is also the life of the dog. But is this not also the case in retail? A shop or a product fits in with the life of a customer, but the customer is the life, the very existence, of a shop. So why are customers treated with so much disdain? Why don't shops and related organisations modify their strategy to the wishes and behaviour of customers?*

Relationships and Loyalty

The relationship with the customer is of crucial importance to a shop. A distinction can be made between the types of relationships, as can be done in everyday life: casual relationships and stable relationships. Relationships based on what parties can offer, and relationships based on communication and contact. The type of relationship that a product or organisation has can be classified into three forms:

- A financial relationship driven by price.

- A social relationship where communication and contact are important. Social media are paramount in this.

- A structural relationship where mutual solidarity is important. This is the case with contracts, outsourcing or these days with new business models such as the subscription system and cloud

---

6   *Harvard Business Review*, July–August 2014, pp. 57–9.

computing. In both cases use plays a central role. And you have to pay for this use.

In the financial relationship price is the flywheel of the relationship. As soon as the price is no longer in line with the expectations of customers they will go to other concepts and suppliers. The low price segment is very much based on this financial bonding. This is why there is such enormous pressure on suppliers to continue to sell at the lowest price. Internet deliveries lead to an increase in costs, resulting in customers choosing to look at other suppliers, as has been shown with Primark. It is very important to keep a close watch on this concept of being cheap. After all, suppliers find it very difficult to always remain the cheapest. Suppliers will try to use various forms of loyalty. A combination of financial relationship and social relationship is also possible. Primark is an example of a company that uses this combination. In addition to the company using the concept of being cheap, it also places itself in a social context: trendy, modern and the feeling of scarcity, along with a different look at fashion. 'Disposable fashion' is an important part of the Primark concept, a concept that actually started at H&M, which responded to fast-changing demands. By selling a frequently changing collection of clothes at affordable prices to young people, a new dimension was added to the fashion world. The idea that the fashion season was limited to two new collections per year was abandoned; a disruption based on buying wishes and quick production possibilities. This concept is also used by Zara, which in its own particular way, uses no advertising, has a clear vision of shop locations and maintains intensive contact with its branches. This allows it to respond quickly to customer demands. All these bonding concepts draw their own particular type of customer. Money can in some cases be the dominant factor, but so too can the social image. It can be the consequence of not having much money, a desired involvement with a particular target group, or tips from friends via social media. Involvement, image and character are important factors for social bonding. Brands in particular provide this social involvement and thereby have a clear and distinctive target group.

New concepts are based more on structural bonding. Cloud computing is an example of this. And so, too, is Amazon Prime, whereby paying a one-off fixed amount exempts you from paying any further shipping costs for the whole year. Subscription forms or models that are used in the software sector are a form of structural bonding. It is difficult to stop these. It may not always be a voluntary bonding, but in this modern context they are a successful business model. Of the three possibilities, the structural model is the most stable. Future business models will be based on bonding through continuity. Social bonding is fickle and greatly depends upon fashion, preferences and personal development, whereas bonding based on price is hard to maintain. New concepts and suppliers, particularly through the Internet, emerge with lower prices. The connection that Alibaba provides between end users and producers whereby the entire supply chain is eliminated, is an example of this. All profit margins have disappeared in order to reach a low retail price.

As there is a great deal of choice in what and where products are sold, human behaviour has become a key factor. The market will as a consequence change to one with shops, shopping centres and products all based on demand. In the past retail model location was very important and accessibility, too, was based on geographic factors. Customers bought their products locally, and had the choice of only a limited number of shops and products. Large retail businesses sought out customers in their own shopping centre. This is a supply-driven buying behaviour that depends upon the local shops and local product ranges. Due to the strength and dominance of large retail chains many shopping areas began to look the same. In the last few years the number of visitors has decreased, due to a different type of buying behaviour and the possibility of being able to buy elsewhere. Another reason is the dullness of the shopping streets and the local council's policy of discouraging visitors from coming to the 'city centre'.

Since 2012 this development has intensified. The reasons are clear: the sharp rise in Internet sales in the non-food segment, the typical shop segment. Customers take more considered decisions regarding their free time and budget. But, in addition, retailers still do not examine the hedonistic aspects enough; there is too little collaboration in making shopping areas more attractive to customers. Altering opening hours is also an increasingly major point of discussion. Retailers want to continue with the traditional opening hours despite the wishes of the customers.

Purchase Flow Analyses

Thanks to increased mobility and the Internet, customers now have a lot more options. Buying at a physical shop or shopping area has become a choice, so that buying patterns now dictate the success of shops and shopping centres. The bonding factors are now becoming a strong buying motive. The bonding factor is an indicator of how pleasant the centre is for the local residents to go shopping there. For daily shopping bonding tends to be much higher than with non-daily purchases. Bonding will also vary considerably according to the type of product. For a centre this is essential information for its general layout and planning, but it is also important for a centre to develop a marketing strategy to increase the bonding.

But the Internet is not the only cause of this. New buying behaviour also plays a major role as previously indicated. Shops have to be enjoyable places to visit, and if the shops in the town or area are not enjoyable to visit people will simply go to other towns or areas which are more pleasant. This will, as a result, decrease the bonding factor as well as the influx of expenditure by non-residents. The various responsible parties: local councils, real estate developers and retailers have to work together to create a targeted marketing plan to make the shopping centre fun and attractive so as to attract and bond customers. The competition is intense and different from before. A good purchase flow measurement, carried out at regular intervals, is essential to keep one's finger on the pulse. At least once per year or, better still, once every six months so that the results of promotions and activities can be measured immediately and therefore adjusted if necessary. The strategy must be aimed at turning the purchase flows towards one's own shopping area. The purchase motives of the local residents and the attractiveness for potential buyers from other municipalities and tourists lie at the basis of this. If successful, a sufficient economic foundation will be created in order to maintain a fun and pleasant centre. If the purchase flows cannot be directed towards the shops then the centre will have to decrease in size, modify the products on offer and perhaps the shopping centre will even have to go altogether. This would, however, have major consequences for the quality of life in the local area, the revenue produced by property tax and the value of the local premises. It is incomprehensible that despite this economic threat there is no longer any collaboration between the interested parties.

Consequences in the Market

The purchase flow analysis reveals three segments in the market: a low price segment with its own rhythm, low prices, and often time-related products. Batch sales can form part of this. These products are often one-offs, costs are kept as low as possible, profit margins are small and profits are made by selling large volumes. This low price segment is becoming increasingly powerful due to social acceptance and good value for money. It is also important that customers believe that they are not paying a penny too much. In addition to the low prices, there is also a clear social bonding. Primark, Zara, H&M as well as Lidl and Aldi have in actual fact become quite sexy. By saving on purchases, money can be spent elsewhere on other products such as mobile phones, games, the

Internet or entertainment. Customers tend to make choices based on whether they can save costs and feel they belong. The pressure on the discretionary income is also a factor in the choices made. In most cases the Internet will have a fairly modest role in this segment (a website instead of a webshop). Primark does show, however, that it is important to keep a watchful eye on the social concept. The website provides a lot of information on the social character of Primark; the campaigns against child labour and the exploitation of workers in Bangladesh. It also publicises that Primark has donated a great deal of money to the victims of Rana Plaza after it collapsed.

In addition to this financial bonding, there is also a strong need for social bonding; to be able to set yourself apart and to belong to a target group of your choosing. Brand experience and brand image are important factors here. Customers are attracted by the imaginary values, the feeling of being able to belong to a particular group. This buying behaviour is strongly initiated by the individualisation in society, the unravelling of old structures and target groups and the need for identification. In this segment, too, the Internet plays a limited role. Websites and clips often provide a good feeling, atmosphere and inspiration. Both segments are strong and growing at the moment. *Due to the different buying behaviour, the customer chooses for a particular segment more*

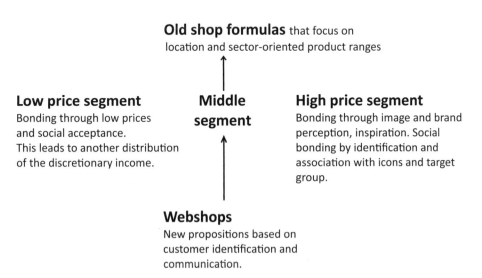

The battle for the middle segment in the market.
A segment that will be dominated by webshops, hybrid shops.

Old shop formulas that focus on
location and sector-oriented product ranges

Low price segment
Bonding through low prices
and social acceptance.
This leads to another distribution
of the discretionary income.

Middle
segment

High price segment
Bonding through image and brand
perception, inspiration. Social
bonding by identification and
association with icons and target
group.

Webshops
New propositions based on
customer identification and
communication.

Figure 9.1   Competitive strategies for different segments

consciously, high or low, and for certain shopping areas. Retailers would need to develop a good Internet proposition based on a hybrid concept for a particular segment (focus), as is successfully done by the department store Bijenkorf (part of Selfridges). The number of shops can therefore be reduced as the Internet provides a good complementary alternative. What's more, much more work would have to be carried out on the brand, the identity and authenticity. The middle segment is a very difficult position for retailers, as they are often too slow to respond and hold onto the old structures and old retail model for too long. This is a position without any prospect, as is also reflected by the current problems in the retail sector.

Loyalty Systems

The wish to bond with customers is nothing new. The local grocer always used to give that little bit extra with the shopping, after all, people are basically people and savings programmes are nothing new either. In the 1990s, however, savings programmes became somewhat more sophisticated due to the application of technology. Air Miles and Flying Dutchman made use of unbooked facilities such as airplane seats and bungalows at Center Parcs for which customers could save by shopping at participating shops. The secret behind these formulas was that it involved 'necessary' purchases, through which points could be saved automatically. On top of this, there was leverage with the saving goal. Air Miles bought the empty bungalows and empty airplane seats cheap, whilst customers had the perception that they were given as a valuable gift (the perception of the standard sale price). Other loyalty programmes never reached the success of these programmes, in particular because people saved for physical products. What's more, customers had to save up for a relatively long period of time for the gift. Even if these products were purchased at cost price there is still a bottom level. With the 'empty' seats and unbooked bungalows there is no bottom. What is actually the value of an empty seat? The airplane would fly anyway.

The loyalty programmes of webshops are usually invisible to customers. Direct communication, specific offers based on customer behaviour, are so individual that customers often do not realise that special rates are being used for good customers. The communication often takes place at times when the customer needs just that little bit of extra incentive to buy. Here a loyalty system is an integral part of the total proposition; actually an individualisation of the old marketing instruments. This is possible thanks to the knowledge webshops have of their individual customers. And this knowledge will only increase in the coming years due to the growth of Internet sales and better analysis systems.

The current loyalty systems in the physical world still have physical products as a savings goal. But these days you can buy so much more cheaply online that it no longer seems worth the effort to save up for products, particularly if you have to do this for months. Saving up for airplane tickets is no longer interesting due to low-cost airlines such as Easy Jet, Ryanair and Vueling. Customers simply want to have the feeling that they have managed to get a good deal at that very moment. A savings programme for discounts no longer fits in with this. Instant gratification, an immediate advantage, is essential for the success of a loyalty programme and for customer bonding.

Almost all loyalty programmes relate to a shop or a retail chain in order to increase the bonding with the shop in question. In the most favourable case customer bonding is stimulated at the shop. The points can be saved at any branch, so no bonding is created with the shopping area itself. The question is whether this sort of programme actually leads to extra purchases. It remains an old concept; the shop and the savings programme. If the shop is in the middle segment, then purchases can be carried out less expensively on the Internet or at low-cost shops. Of course, customers will always take their stamp cards with them and collect their points. It does not take any extra effort or cost, but it will no longer lead to any significant bonding. Such programmes are not really relevant for low-cost shops. They would only lead to higher costs; the loyalty and customer bonding is after all already included in their low price. It is also not interesting for the higher segment, as the bonding there involves association and bonding with the brand or shop.

Services, image, experience are the loyalty factors for the high segment. It is the shopping areas that must attract, bond and reward customers. The purchase flow analyses clearly show this. The purchase flows must continue or be directed towards a particular shopping area. Many factors play a role in this, such as accessibility, (free) parking, layout of the public space, but in particular personal bonding factors. Ultimately it is about the customer spending money. And in order to achieve this, customers must:

- Feel comfortable, happy and relaxed.

- Feel they are valued, rewarded and pleasantly surprised.

- Stay longer in the shopping centre. The longer customers stay in the shopping centre, the more money is spent there.

Shops are not distinctive enough to attract and bond customers independently. That's why there has to be collaboration within the shopping area. Bars and restaurants will also have to contribute to the conviviality of the shopping centre. Pleasant and attractive bars and restaurants attract visitors, provide a pleasant experience and help to keep customers in the shopping centre for longer. This stimulates a willingness to buy and lowers buying thresholds.

The principles of the old loyalty programmes, and the lessons learnt from these, provide a good basis for new loyalty programmes. These should ensure that customers become truly motivated to go to physical shops. They must also help to create a bond with the shopping area, include services within the loyalty concept and provide a similar sort of leverage between costs and perceived rewards. Of course, the available technology has to be used to the full; so this includes the smartphone, the Internet, databases and iBeacons. The days of the stamp card are well behind us and the use of customer cards, though popular in the 1990s, is now a thing of the past. It is sometimes incorrectly suggested that this would therefore exclude the older target group. Figures examining the penetration of the Internet, however, show a rapid growth of Internet use and smartphones amongst the older generation.

Marketing is no longer aimed at selling (the realisation of a transaction). Marketing needs to be increasingly focused on motivating and bonding customers. The desired buying behaviour has to be stimulated, and we should certainly not see any banning of supply-oriented facilities such as opening hours or shop locations. Local councils are responsible for ensuring a pleasant town centre, property owners for a pleasant shopping centre, and retailers for a likewise pleasant shop. And jointly they are responsible for attracting, bonding and motivating customers. Any marketing efforts should be a joint effort directed at individual customers with the focus on the individual buying behaviour. The old marketing instruments, the 4Ps, have to be replaced by a marketing mix of customer-based instruments such as communication, commitment and connection. Shops have to realise that shopping has become a choice and is no longer a necessity. Responding to the new buying behaviour is essential if shops are to survive. This means a disruption to all facets of business and private life.

PART 3
Learning From Practice

The past is a guideline for the future

You can not change the past but you can change your future

Look at opportunities not at threats

Chapter 10

Innovation or Disruption?
The Reality

It is of course obvious that when society changes, as well as customers and their buying behaviour and motives, existing retailers also have to adapt to the new situation. Holding onto old structures and habits is not the way forward.

The changes that are necessary in retail are based on supporting the purchase the moment it is made, whether from the home or in the shop. These changes can take the form of shops on the Internet, technological applications in shops and shopping areas and, lastly, adapting the retail concept.

Shops on the Internet

The major disruptor with a shop on the Internet is Amazon.com. Amazon started in the 1990s and changed retail through its strong focus on customer value. The ambition to be the largest, the best and to offer the best deals became ingrained throughout the company. As 'first mover' they became the largest retailer in America, and through their margins, service, product range and, in particular, their prices they attacked the existing retailers. This led to considerable changes in shops and the products and services they offered. Many shops and chain stores disappeared or had to adapt very quickly in order to survive, often in slimmed down versions (Barnes & Noble and Walmart are the largest and most well-known examples). We still see this process going on right now. We also see shopping centres disappearing, the legacy of no longer appealing to customers. And if shops lose their appeal, something has to be done. Using the available technology can help in this, such as lighting, iBeacons, smartphone support and videos, as can the support provided by bars and restaurants, entertainment and perhaps also sport facilities. In America new shopping centres are increasingly often combined with nursing homes and medical health centres. The (free) parking facilities are shared. The attraction of the shopping centre is also due to the fact that the centre houses a nursing home or a medical health centre which people may need to visit, so that customers can do their shopping while there. Out-of-town, multifunctional facilities such as the familiar outlet centres, also attract customers. If shopping centres fail to attract customers they will continue to dwindle. In America shopping centres are under pressure; in England the town centres are struggling. By adding a new dimension to town centres in the form of bars and restaurants, culture, theatre and small traditional shops, these town centres can once more be attractive to visitors. This is also possible in the Netherlands if clear direction is given. In America, Amazon has given customers an alternative: low prices, new facilities and, above all, buying convenience. Customers are pampered by Amazon. With its webshop this new entrant changed the structure of retail; and not taking part in this has proven disastrous for existing shops. The current focus of Amazon is to deliver quickly in populated areas. This will only intensify the attack on shops. Making deliveries using drones and experimenting with one-hour deliveries are already showing this. These experiments are, of course, taking place in densely-populated cities in America, such as Silicon Valley and New York City, in large cities and sometimes in Seattle, the home base of Amazon. If successful, the rollout will be very simple, certainly in a densely populated country such as the Netherlands. In the Netherlands, Bol.com has had the same influence as Amazon has had in America. As was the case in America, there have been many followers in the Netherlands which has helped to make the Internet a fully developed channel for shopping. This development was reinforced by the lack of response from retailers. It was only at a later stage that webshops were set up, but it was often too late. Shops have to find a way to attract customers once again if they want customers to buy from them.

The webshops' focus on logistics has been an attack on the sales of physical shops, whereby for Amazon this has been a defence against Alibaba. Ordering online via Alibaba may well be cheap and efficient, but logistics (waiting for the order) is its weakness.

In addition to the shop, Amazon has efficient facilities, payment systems, web services and analyses (data). Amazon opened a marketplace for retailers, which allows them to see precisely which products are selling well and which are not, where the profit is being made and identifies buying patterns. This leads again to more knowledge of customers and their buying processes. Amazon claims that it can use these analyses to predict up to 70 per cent of the purchases a week in advance. Experiments to bring the expected order closer to the customer up to the moment the order is placed ensures speedy deliveries. Amazon is highly innovative and has changed the retail sector for good. Other webshops have followed these developments, which has further increased the effects of these changes. In the coming years Amazon is expected to grow by an average of 20 per cent each year in America. The benefits provided by Amazon and other webshops are the savings on margins by buying directly from manufacturers, limited stock risks, a great deal of knowledge of the buying processes and direct communication. To counter this, the old retail model can only offer local shops and the physical availability of products, but at higher costs and often also at higher prices. Are customers still motivated enough to pay this?

Retailers Really Must Adapt[1]

It is possible, however, for retailers to effectively motivate customers to visit their shops. And it starts with the shop itself. The retailer needs to get to know his customers, use new media and communicate actively with customers. This has already been explained and discussed in detail in the book *The End of Shops*. In addition, partnership is also important. Local councils, property owners, shops and suppliers must work together to develop a model that is actually interesting enough to entice customers to buy. This could take the form of outlet centres, where shops and entertainment are located at the same place. Town centres would then offer culture, bars and restaurants, and appropriate shops: often smaller, fun and traditional shops. This structure is also discussed in the book *The End Of Shops?*[2] The response to these proposals was based on the threat to existing shops and shopping centres, their lack of skill in dealing with the shrinkage and the problems that would arise with existing business models. Due to the defensive attitude of shopkeepers, chain stores and interest groups, valuable time to respond to this new buying behaviour has been lost. As a result, the problems for shops and shopping centres have only become greater. And it is perhaps now even too late for certain cities or areas.

> *Invention is in our DNA and technology is the fundamental tool we wield to improve every aspect of the experience we provide our customers. We still have a lot to learn. But it's still Day 1 (Jeff Bezos, CEO, Amazon.com).*

Hointer, a shop in Seattle is experimenting with using new technology to get to know customers, and to communicate directly with them, even in the shop and the fitting room. A customer's own smartphone forms the basis for this

---

1   Some of these examples have been taken from Stern (2014).
2   Molenaar (2011).

communication; interactive mirrors will be placed in the shop at a later stage. All items of clothing have a NFC tag, which allows customers to see the product information. Hointer's aim is to inform customers better, to save on sales staff and to also sell related products with the purchase.

The key point in this change is the utilisation of the effective floor space. The stock room takes up only 10 per cent of the space, with the shop itself 90 per cent. The smartphone is becoming ever more important in the buying process; it is the link between the supplier (shop) and the customer, and makes a multichannel approach possible. At Hointer the prices are controlled at a central database. All the articles have a NFC chip and QR code. By activating this code with the smartphone, the prices of the article are shown. This allows prices to be changed quickly (dynamic pricing) and enables personal pricing. In this way, customers can be stimulated to buy more articles: longer cash till receipts and a higher basket value. It is possible for customers to control the entire (buying) process themselves with the smartphone including payment through their own smartphone.

The application of technology can also be linked with the product. The customer can design his own product or add his own design to a product. We see this, for example, with *The Kase*, started by the founder of Pixmania. The shop, which is based in Paris, sells covers for smartphones and tablets. Customers are able to design the cover themselves by using interactive terminals to produce their own layout and text. In just a short time, five shops were opened in France (2012) and two in Singapore. A rapid expansion on the Internet was predicted. In August 2013, some 114 shops of Phonehouse were taken over in France, which allowed the products to be geared even better towards the customer. The combination of buying a smartphone and a cover coupled with a personal design is a logical one.

In Amsterdam on the Kalverstraat high street, Marks & Spencer shows that the integration of technology in shops can certainly bring about benefits. Everything in the Marks & Spencer product range can be bought, despite there being only a limited choice available in the shop itself. The products are sold by means of terminals and interactive mirrors. This allows a rapid market penetration, there are no stock risks and only a small floor surface area is required. It is actually a variant to the shopping on the Internet model, but with personal service and support without the high costs of a traditional shop. There is a combination of foodstuffs and non-daily products. This makes it easier to enter the Dutch market more quickly, whilst at the same time meeting the wishes of the typical shoppers on the Kalverstraat. The shop includes a range of foods that respond to the wishes of quick buyers; ready-made meals, lunch products, as well as a non-food product range, are targeted towards the same type of buyers or target group. The sales staff have an iPad that allows them to help the customers with their purchases straightaway. This shop is clearly an experiment to see whether this will catch on, whether the Dutch market is perhaps interested in having this chain of stores once more. There are now new Marks & Spencer shops in Amsterdam and The Hague.

Chilli Beans is a concept store where customers are able to try out all the products there and share their experiences immediately through social media. Many products are handmade, based on the individual wishes of customers. The customers are also treated to entertainment events on Saturday, restaurants and bars and new eye-catching products. They also have a 'fast fashion' approach whereby they update, for example, the collection of sunglasses every 15 days. Inspiration is also offered through the many video panels, the interaction terminals and the connection with social media. The key concepts are fun and interactivity. They are therefore clearly driven by hedonistic factors, but also supported by new technological applications. Thanks to the frequently changing product range, customers soon come back. We have seen the same approach with Zara and Primark.

In addition to its own brand shops, H&M also has & Other Stories and COS. & Other Stories is a new H&M brand whereby a new collection that differs from the H&M collection is displayed. The shop does have a similar price perception of value for money. They make use of social media and blogs to understand what customers want as well as what they expect in shops. This is then translated into brands, product range and the shop layout. The product range is positioned between H&M and its own brand COS, which is a more expensive shop. There is a strong focus on the wishes of the customers. In some ways it resembles the webshop ASOS which sells products with which a customer wants to be associated because friends or celebrities wear the articles as well.

The Burberry Flagship store in Regent Street in London is also well known. It employs a unique concept which is all about the experience. Burberry refers to a 'retail theatre'. The layout is in an old building with atmosphere and history, as well as a limited number of products kept in the store, all of which helps to give it a relaxed feel. There is an extra service provided by the staff which is to help you in your purchases, and then they quickly retrieve the articles while customers have a drink waiting on a Chesterfield. This is all part of the experience. Large video screens with fashion shows and appropriate music are a feast for the eyes and ears. The products are given an NFC tag, so that not only can you see yourself in the mirror, but the other two mirrors also show a fashion show with the product and a video over the manufacture process.

Burberry is naturally not a cheap shop, but the aim of becoming a sexy brand once more has turned out to be a success. The sales have increased not only in London but also around the world. Thanks to its image and the many videos of the shop in London coupled to YouTube and social media, considerable involvement was created amongst customers. Burberry used technology to breathe new life into the shops, from music and rich video content on large internal and external screens to the iPads used by the sales staff. Customer profiles are also made and the sales staff can refer to these during their contact with the customers. Online, offline and irrespective of which shop, all the data is collected and can be seen immediately by the person having contact with the customer. 'We wanted customers to come into our world, the dreamworld that we created for them', explains CEO Angela Ahrendts. There are now more digital contacts than contacts through other media; 60 per cent of customers buy online but then collect their order at the shop. 'If the shop does not look or feel like the webshop, then you are no longer a serious brand for your customers', warns Angela Ahrendts.[3]

There are, of course, plenty of examples of retailers that do respond to the wishes of customers, the new buying behaviour or the application of technology in all its forms. For smaller shops it is not the technology that is important, but the product range, service, customer bonding and personal aspects. The costs of shops have to be looked at anew, as well as the number of metres of effective floor space and in relation to that the revenue per square metre. These retail gems can clearly be seen in many towns, which as a result have their own particular dynamism and appeal. Bonding, surprising and motivating customers are key to every shop.

Other Applications of Technology

In addition to the adaptations to the shops, there also has to be collaboration between the shops in the shopping centre. A number of shops can act as crowd pullers, but it is important for the entire area to be attractive and appealing. Increasing numbers of (IT) suppliers come up with loyalty systems for attracting customers to shops. These systems are often based on old ideas: saving points

---

3   This case can be seen on YouTube and other sources, as described in *Leading Digital*, pp. 31ff.

for gifts, discounts or perhaps cultural organisations or sport clubs. These concepts date back to the 1990s, and were successful for a while. But now it takes more to attract and bond customers. A shop in itself is not appealing enough. And do customers feel the need to be loyal?

Are the savings goals actually attractive enough if the customer can already buy everything on the Internet, usually at better prices than at the shop? Retailers should just work out what the rationale is for customers, how much they buy, how much they save and what it yields. If the supplier (retailer) spends 3 per cent on loyalty (this was the rule of thumb in the 1990s) then the customer can save €210 per year. At other retail chains there is a maximum savings of up to €250. Still saving up for a year, buying everything from these shops in order to save a maximum of €250 per year. On the basis of this, the same calculation can still be made. How much does an average customer spend on non-food, and how much in a particular shop? It has very quickly become clear that this is not interesting for a small shop, particularly considering the additional costs. Customers really are no longer willing to save for months, or even years, for discounts or for a particular article. With an average expenditure of €500 per year at a particular shop, some €15 is saved in the knowledge that it is always cheaper on the Internet. At present the amount a shop is willing to spend on loyalty is still a maximum of 3 per cent and often less (sometimes even 0 per cent). The social cohesion aspect, where customers may save for culture or the sports club, is not interesting either. Customers are too individualistic as well as too fickle for this.

Loyalty as a Basis for Physical Shopping Centres

The basic principles of a new loyalty system focus on buying motives, attracting customers to city centres and shopping centres and bonding customers in the centre. This will have to lead to a redirection of cash flows. Collaboration between shops and bars and restaurants is essential for achieving these aims. Shops are no longer attractive enough to compete independently in the middle segment. The competition with the Internet, other shopping areas and other suppliers (shops) is too great for this. Also, the motives for shopping (necessity has made way for conviviality) have changed. And the principles of the ease of saving up, the system's readiness for the future and the registration for direct communication also apply. All this leads to knowledge about customers, which is crucial in order to compete successfully. Points issued at the shop, can, for example, be redeemed (cashed in) at bars and restaurants. By working closely together, an attractive loyalty system can meet the required conditions. In the

Dutch town of Boxtel shops, bars and restaurants tried out such a concept in November 2014. Each Saturday for every €20 spent the retailer issued a coupon that could be used for a free cup of coffee and a cake. The coupon was only valid on the same day, and a maximum of four were given for each purchase. The aim was to attract customers to the shop by giving them this reward, to bind them by offering them something at a bar or restaurant, thereby offering an additional experience. This particular promotion had very positive results. Of the 74 shops, 56 participated in this promotion, and on Saturdays customers came to the city centre specifically for this. An average of more than 400 coupons were redeemed every Saturday. Outdoor cafés were full of happy customers. And let's not forget, a happy customer always buys more. It was disappointing, however, that there were still retailers who did not participate in this, which led to irritation amongst customers. A clear lack of understanding of customers and customer motives is shown in the comment from one retailer in particular: 'We can serve coffee to our customers ourselves'. Negative messages soon appeared on Twitter and Facebook about this. This type of promotion can only be successful if customers are rewarded immediately, if everyone participates collectively and the promotion is publicised widely, not only through the media, but also by the retailer and in the shop. It was a great pity to see retailers hanging the posters at the very bottom of the shop window next to those of the local football club or theatre company. Retailers, too, have to acquire more knowledge of customer motives, and must be willing to attract customers. Simply waiting passively for customers to come to you (or not as the case may be) is asking for problems. The system was attractive because retailers spent a maximum of 3 per cent of their turnover on loyalty, the bars or restaurants reimbursed the cost price and customers had the perception that they were given €5 worth of drink and food for free (therefore a perception of 25 per cent of the purchase price!).

An increasing number of loyalty systems also appear on websites or via apps. Points can be saved, for example, for discounts, local sport clubs or cultural activities; but as mentioned before, people are no longer really interested in this. These systems are sold to retailers, but they can actually have a counter-productive effect on shopping centres and shopping areas. Customers want more stimulating, immediate rewards. They are more individual, more self-seeking and better informed than ever before. Customers know that it is easier and cheaper to buy on the Internet and can have their purchases delivered to their home for free as an extra service. With the loyalty system, shops therefore have to offer and think of a better reward. The customer's hedonist motivation (surprise, inspire and reward me) must form the basic principle as was clearly shown in the promotion in Boxtel.

A change is required in the retail sector, a change based on customer motives and customer processes. It is essential to attract customers to the shopping area and to reward them. Serving your own coffee and not collaborating with local bars and restaurants shows a clear misunderstanding and misjudgement of customers' wishes, and will certainly not entice customers to buy. The challenge for retailers is to apply marketing in a different way, to maintain direct contact with customers and, above all, to motivate them to buy in their shops. A passive attitude will be the death of retailers. Active entrepreneurship is required for a successful future.

Tempting scents

Feel safe, secure and nostalgic: Talcum powder.
Be more alert: Peppermint, citrus.
Relax: Lavender, vanilla.
Perceive a room as smaller: Barbecue smoke.
Perceive a room as bigger: Apple.
Buy a house: Freshly baked cake or apple pie.
Browse longer and spend more in shop: Floral and citrus scent.

Tempting lighting

Warm lighting leads to customers browsing in the shop for longer, whereas cold lighting can be used to entice customers to make quicker decisions, leading to a higher turnover rate of customers (busy times). The till receipts increase by an average of 2%.

Dynamic light (blue light) at Schiphol airport shops led to 12% more stopping power and 3% more sales. In addition, it led to a change in customers' walking behaviour (more to the middle of the shop)

Tempting sounds

Experiments in the 1980s at supermarkets and restaurants showed that slow tempo music led to slower customer behaviour. Customers browsed in the shop for longer or stayed longer at the table in a restaurant, which in turn led to more sales.

Integral Loyalty System Stimulates Sales

The purpose of a loyalty system is to motivate customers to buy. It should *attract, motivate and bond* customers. Old concepts were developed for particular shops or brands. The focus was often solely on the transaction, where purchases were rewarded with points. The points could then be redeemed for discounts or free products. People had to save for weeks, months, even years. Often the purpose of these programmes was not altogether clear; a savings card that offered a 10 per cent discount after eating at the restaurant 10 times? Other variants used plastic cards. This was quite sexy in the late 1980s, but they are simply a nuisance now. A loyalty card, however, such as that of a department store has a direct purpose (payment) and provides immediate privileges that go beyond simply saving for discounts: special evenings, privilege to be amongst the first at sales and promotions as well as other facilities that bond and motivate the customer. This makes customers feel special. The department store should have a strong brand with a strong *social bonding*. Other shops that do not have this bonding can only offer a financial bonding, which doesn't last: discounts after all can be found everywhere.

Social bonding is essential for shopping areas to attract customers, to motivate them and create a bond. Social aspects are important in this, as are the previously-mentioned hedonistic aspects such as experience, inspiration, pampering and convenience. Loyalty systems that are based on social bonding have to meet a number of conditions:

- They have to offer more than just discounts. Discounts reduce the margins that have already shrunk and lead to cannibalisation. Customers will also make comparisons with other suppliers, as they do on the Internet. It is always cheaper online, so why save for a discount?

- They have to respond to social and hedonistic needs. Customers first have to feel happy if they are to buy more and browse in the shopping area for longer. Bars and restaurants play a crucial role in this. People with smiles on their faces are more likely to buy.

- The system has to be highly useful so that the app appears on the first page of Google and then it becomes an integral part of the buying process, the customer journey.

- The system must be convenient, respond to individual customer wishes and represent value.

In order to be successful, the loyalty system must consist of a combination of a savings programme, a location-based programme, a payment facility and a communications/marketing system. The technology is based on a smartphone app and involves connecting the loyalty system with the cash till. If necessary, a small device provides this connection. All interaction takes place automatically via the smartphone and the payment system such as at the cash till or online. But the technology can make or break the implementation, which must be convenient, quick and above all glitch-free. Finalising the sales transaction at the cash till has to be quick; a few seconds can often cause irritation if there is a queue.

The Principle

Retailers issue points when purchases are made. The customer receives these points on his account, which allows him to go to a bar or restaurant for a free cup of coffee, lunch or dinner, depending on the number of points issued. One point is awarded for every €20 spent. This one point is already enough for a free cup of coffee, five points gets the customer a free lunch. In this way, the customer quickly gets the feeling of being treated. But the customer also feels as if he is getting something useful in return. The system is a so-called community system for all participants, shops and bars and restaurants. Together they administer the points, process the payments and finalise the transaction. This is done following specific rules in which the agreements and procedures are set down. The standard principle is that the shops pay €1 for each point issued, and the bar or restaurant is reimbursed at cost price. To the retailer it feels as if they are paying 5 per cent of the turnover to loyalty (€1 euro per €20 sales), but in reality this is approximately 3 per cent as not all the points are cashed in and the sale prices are rounded off. At €18.50 no points are issued and at €32.50 still just one point. This 3 per cent is an average amount that a retailer is willing to pay for loyalty. The bar or restaurant is reimbursed only for the cost price. Of course it wouldn't be right if bars and restaurants were to make a profit at the expense of a retailer.

It turns out that customers actually do spend more time in shopping areas where there are bars and restaurants, to drink more coffee (the first after all is free), also to have lunch or to drink more during lunch (as lunch is free). Bars and restaurants therefore benefit directly from this promotion (on average the turnover increases by 20 per cent). Retailers benefit as well, as customers often get additional small purchases to be able to pay in amounts of €20 as much as possible. In addition, such systems have a certain appeal. The customer does not need to save for long in order to gain a benefit, the recreational buying behaviour is supported and the time spent in the centres is increased. The direct effects are still being measured, but an extra turnover impulse of 15 per cent is expected as was also measured in Veghel and Boxtel as well.

The difference between the value of the points when they are issued (€1) and the value upon collection (€0.25) is an operational cash flow for the collective (the foundation or business association). This revenue can be used to, for example, develop other activities, or to pay for the costs of the system or perhaps to change the financial settlement between the participants (less costs for shops or more revenue for the bars and restaurants). The marketing module also has a website facility, which is direct control of special offers through an app. These activities will only happen if the customer has opted for them. There is a direct link with the Tourist Office information and the city information systems that provide tourists with assistance. Tourists are becoming increasingly important for providing an economic boost, particularly to city centres.

In the second phase, payment will also be part of the system. The payments are primarily aimed at providing direct support to buying behaviour; for example, paying for parking and childcare in order to make shopping more fun and paying for tourist activities. Payments can be made using loyalty points, if necessary with a surcharge if the points are insufficient. The purpose is to make sure customers are not irritated by parking costs or home delivery charges. Local councils are usually not willing to scrap the parking revenue because of the impact it would have on their budget. So, parking is paid for, but costs the customer nothing (or that's what it feels like). Childcare is particularly important at the weekends; while parents do their shopping children are entertained in a play den (perhaps set up in an empty premise). This would stimulate sales and payment could be made using the points.

Lastly, tourists are an important (potential) source of income for many towns and cities. By coming to shop in the city they can take part in some cultural or entertainment activities for free. This helps to make shopping more fun and adds a recreational element, a day out or a weekend break.

In the third phase the total functionality is integrated. This will therefore include payments using the smartphone (also with Internet providers, other banks and new payment forms such as Apple Pay and PayPal), online orders using a smartphone and other facilities that are yet to be developed.

This phased implementation has been deliberately chosen in order to allow customers to get used to the new system, where the focus lies particularly on loyalty. By having a strong focus on loyalty, shops, bars and restaurants will be given an immediate boost and a positive attitude will be created amongst customers. The system is administered by a foundation or business association. This body sets down the rules regarding the financial settlement, communication, expansion, and what to do with the positive cash flow and the points that are not redeemed. Agreements will also be made regarding when the points can be redeemed (preferably at the weekend), when for example promotions can be carried out with double points and how to handle deviating points allocation. It is up to the businesses to determine their rules, but with the aim of *attracting, bonding and motivating customers*. Discounts on products and free products are ineffective tools as they do not really stimulate buying. Suddenly the points have an absolute value. And of course there is still the Internet; it is always cheaper to buy online, so why bother saving?

What Will the Customer Notice with Such a Loyalty System?

Points are collected using the smartphone and then credited to the account automatically through the smartphone. Customers will be able to view their account themselves. The points can be used at bars or restaurants to pay for free coffee, lunch or dinner. Partial payment is also an option. The points can also be used to pay for parking, childcare or home deliveries (phase 2). Payment for all services, location-based services, payment for events, cultural or tourist attractions are also amongst the possibilities (phase 3).

The strength of this application is the required collaboration in the shopping area between retail businesses and the local bars and restaurants. The smartphone is the carrier with which the system can be used daily. In addition, there is the leverage that applies to the benefits: the customer has the perception his coffee is worth €2.50, whilst the participating parties agree to settle for a cost price of €0.25. The system supports the new buying behaviour, stimulates the senses and feelings (pampering), and removes a number of barriers involved in shopping such as parking and children. Home deliveries (for one point) are also among the possibilities; not having to carry your purchases leads to more purchases. All these facilities are necessary in order to stimulate the buying behaviour of customers at shops, and to redirect purchase flows to shop locations. Only then will shops have a future.

The focus will have to be on customers and their motivation. This means that choices need to be made that differ from those that were made traditionally. There has to be collaboration in order to attract customers, and more flexible opening hours are necessary to allow customers to shop at different times. Businesses must:

- Think in terms of loyalty and services, not in terms of transactions.

- Communicate actively, if possible immediately before and during shopping.

- Realise that customers do not come to buy (after all, they can do that anywhere) but come for the experience, to feel inspired and for the sheer fun of it. A cup of coffee in the shop is no longer anything new, but a coupon for a cup of coffee at a nearby bar or restaurant is a totally new experience.

- Make the customer feel special, let the shopping centre or shopping area become a cosy living room and offer more services in partnership than you would be able to do as a retailer on your own.

There is no point in retailers complaining about decreasing turnover and lower profit margins. Nor does it help to complain about what the city council fails to do and about customers who do not want to come to their shop. They should think about what customers want, motivate them, provide services and create a bond with them through loyalty. A new way of thinking is required, in which retailers put themselves in the shoes of the customer. No longer in terms of products or sales but in terms of needs and purchases. They should dare to take action and apply the system to customers. And have a look at webshops to see why they are so appealing to customers, and also at the webshops' weak points, and then turn the focus on shops. Of course many shops will not survive. We need fewer shops, but different shopping locations. To deny this development is beyond question, as the trends are so clear and the consequences of not recognising this so disastrous. Retailers should talk with customers, look at the strong growth in online sales and the ever-increasing numbers of vacant shop premises. Realise that the reason for further declining numbers of visitors to shopping areas is because customers are making different choices about what they do with their free time. These developments must form the basis for new adaptations and for a new type of shopping area, because shops are important for the viability of towns and communities. This is the responsibility of all parties concerned, but the local city councils first and foremost.

Chapter 11

Cornerstones of Change, on the Road to the Future

The future is built upon a number of cornerstones of change whereby the behaviour of people (their buying behaviour) is the most important. This buying behaviour is influenced by technology, personal circumstances, international developments and economic causes. We have looked in detail at how it was, how it is and how it can be in the future. Old structures and old power patterns are proving to be recalcitrant, and uncertainty is leading to a denial of the ongoing developments. But change always leads to uncertainty, as success is never guaranteed and because there are always those with interests in the old structures who only point out the negative sides of the changes. In actual fact, we can see an ongoing power struggle, where the old parties in power will defend their interests until the very end with all the resources at their disposal. They will frenetically hold onto old shopping centres, to town centres that were developed 50 years ago, and to old sources of income such as municipal land taxes, parking fees and administrative charges. A supply chain that was once effective is now being dismantled by new patterns. The use of drones is met with resistance for the time being as aviation regulations do not yet allow for this. Uber is being blocked because this is against the interests of taxi companies, and orders from webshops outside the EU are being taxed with VAT and import duties. All these restrictions, however, can only slow down developments; they cannot stop them. Customers will not be held back, they will find their own way. Countries that are less rigid in responding to these changes will have a head start and thereby immediately exert pressure on other countries to join in. The Sunday opening hours of shops is perhaps a good example of this. This was first seen in the US, then in England, after which most other European countries followed suit. It will be the same with the Internet and technological applications, but only faster, much faster.

Why Do Customers Want Change?

People these days lead different lives than those a decade ago. In part due to the recession people have learnt how to deal with uncertainty, to not look too far ahead, and to make well-considered choices based on their individual needs and wishes. We have chosen not to take on too many commitments and to remain flexible in mind and behaviour in order to be able to respond to changes more quickly. Single-person households, variable employment contracts and the growing number of freelance workers are examples of this. Also the growing demand for rented accommodation instead of house buying is a sign of this flexibility and desire for less fixed costs.

These choices are leading to an increasing demand for smaller accommodation in other places (towns and cities). Urbanisation is on the rise, the reverse of 40 years ago when everybody wanted a house with a garden for the family. And suppliers are responding to this. *AH to go* of the large Dutch supermarket chain Albert Heijn facilitates these consumers with smaller packs and the possibility of doing the shopping quickly. In England, Marks & Spencer is focusing ever more on these new consumers with smaller packs of food and ready-made meals. Increasing numbers of bars and cafés that did not previously serve meals are now providing this service. We are also seeing more fast food restaurants providing more dressed-up meals. These meals are practical and quick, but the surroundings are better than the normal fast food suppliers. Long tables with magazines and the possibility of eating at a food bar are an attractive option for the new singles.

Increasingly more time is being spent on recreation, socialising, hobbies and often also on work. The fact that people have less time is one of the main reasons why they buy on the Internet. Online buying is quick, it is clear and the orders are delivered to the home. And if you are not going to be at home then collection points provide a good solution. Physical restrictions play an ever-decreasing role. Buying via tablet, smartphone or computer has become common practice, and it can be done practically anywhere. The consumer of today is becoming increasingly fickle, quick and impatient. Everything has to be possible and it has to happen *now*. The applications of technology, such as location-based services, triggers and apps support this wish. Consumers are finding it increasingly difficult to do without these new tools and gadgets. Consumers are willing to spend more and more money on these, with all the resulting budgetary consequences.

For a number of years now discretionary income has not risen, yet consumers want to buy all these new products, to keep up with the latest developments and technological innovations. In the last few years we have seen a shift in consumer expenditure; young people tend no longer to buy a car, as this takes a large chunk out of their budgets and results in too many fixed costs. Customised transport, public transport and taxis are more pleasant. This choice has freed up more of their budget. But the costs of everyday provisions are also seen as taking a chunk out of their wallet. So customers look for cheaper alternatives. This expenditure can be kept down by not buying from the market leader, not buying any brand products and through a slight shift in what is bought. We can thank Lidl and Aldi for this reduced strain on budgets. Other supermarkets have followed these price reductions, which have benefited customers of course. This movement is not restricted to the Netherlands, but can be seen throughout Western Europe, with Great Britain leading the way.

Clothing, too, can be cheaper and yet still remain fashionable. A few years ago the fashion industry began to feel the pressure due to online sales. Not all the clothing was sold in one season and this led to many discounts during and prior to the sales periods. The response of the fashion industry was revealing. Not two collections per year, in the summer and in the winter, but many more collections throughout the year, sometimes as many as 12. Zara and H&M led the way in this change. Thanks to their many new collections it was possible to produce smaller numbers, which led to fewer surplus articles when not everything was sold. Sales were also stimulated because customers did not want to walk around in something from an old collection. This led to the new trend of disposable fashion. This is a fashion trend whereby styles follow one another in quick succession, which means that the clothes don't have to last or be worn for long. Low prices coupled with constantly changing styles result in many sales at low prices and in a quickly repeating buying behaviour. Primark led the way in this trend of providing inexpensive clothes that were not designed to be worn for years on end and that were affordable for everyone.

This fashion trend was initiated by Internet sales of fashion articles. Low prices, home deliveries and being able to try the clothes on at home were appealing aspects and led to a decrease in shop sales. The current development of disposable fashion at low prices provides an answer to these online sales. The small margins cannot absorb the extra cost associated with online sales; the costs of the webshop, the costs of packing and shipping were simply too high and would otherwise lead to higher prices. The prices in the shops are so competitive that the customer has to decide whether to buy inexpensive articles in the shop or more expensive articles online, but with the convenience of doing so at home. This is certainly a major change. No longer are webshops with their low prices the disruptor; but rather it is these new shop concepts that are causing the disruption, by offering even lower prices and thereby attacking the webshops at cost level.

Due to the shift in buying behaviour and the new shop concepts, more room has been created in the customer's budget. This room is used to facilitate the new behaviour and to pay for the new technological purchases. Smartphones, digital television and the Internet have now acquired an unassailable place within everyone's budget (approximately 9 per cent). It is after all technology that has led to these changes with customers and in the product ranges. But the consequences extend much further.

What Role does Technology Play in These Changes?

Technology facilitates the changes and stimulates new applications. Internet applications have been the great disruptor of the last few years. Computers, for example, continue to double in capacity every two years, and in turn make increasingly more applications possible. Large databases can be analysed within a few seconds. Customer recognition using face recognition software is possible within the blink of an eye, customers can be tracked everywhere and direct communication is possible at all times. Whatever customers do as individuals, wherever they are and whatever they want, everything is known and can be controlled. The technology is integrated within the daily lives of people and supports their behaviour. This provides ever more possibilities and requires further radical modifications to existing structures. In the early years, webshops were initially sufficient to support the buying behaviour. Now, however, they are no longer up to the task. A webshop was no more than a shop on the Internet where people could buy things 24/7. After the purchase, the orders had to be delivered to the home. In the beginning this could be within a number of days, but this is now carried out increasingly faster with deliveries being made even on the same day. But people still have to wait.

In addition to the rapid growth in computer capacity, there is also miniaturisation. Everything is becoming smaller, with increasingly more new possible applications as a result. Chips are attached to the products, inside a watch or even in the body. Terrabyte storage memories on a single square centimetre, carrying unbelievably vast data files that tell you everything about someone's life, health, behaviour, environment, in addition to all sorts of control tools for location data, profiles and devices. Everything can be controlled, monitored and initiated. The world of the Internet has only just begun, but the patterns can already be seen. People can know, influence and direct everything. People are the dominant factor that determines which developments will be successful and which undesired.

Why Are Old Structures Still Being held On To?

All these new technological possibilities did not exist a few years ago, but now form an integral part of our lives and must become an integral part of our society and business life. But certain structures and patterns have already existed since before the developments of the last few years. They therefore really belong to another era. Things that are now possible were not possible then. These structures and processes were designed without these technologies, and now come across as out dated. This leads to irritation and excessively high costs. Disposable fashion is an example of how disruption can change the process. But also marketplaces, portals, collectors and new facilitators can change structures and processes. At a marketplace you can buy from the manufacturer or supplier directly. And via a portal you get to know the entire product range and a great deal of information is available to assist you in your purchasing. A collector brings supply and demand together, perhaps based on old systems such as shops. But new connections are also possible as shown by Uber.

If it is possible, however, to efficiently connect supply and demand to one another whereby manufacturers (and brands) can supply directly to customers, why then is a supply chain necessary? This supply chain was traditionally used to transport goods throughout the world, from raw materials to semi-finished to finished products via the importer to the wholesaler, from the wholesaler to the retailer, and then finally to the consumer. A very long chain indeed, with each link wanting to charge on costs and make a profit. This supply chain was useful, but has now become far too expensive. If manufacturers and brands deliver directly to their customers, who want to buy directly online, the costs are much lower and so is the final price. If manufacturers choose to also have a few physical shops (such as outlet centres) they can also make considerable savings, at the very least on the margins of the retailer. Is this then crazy or undesirable? If customers prefer to buy directly from the manufacturer, online or through an outlet centre, why then deny them this possibility? Could it be because the supply chain needs to be protected, with high retail prices as a result? If shops can no longer provide customers with that extra something, or meet the wishes of customers, then these shops no longer fulfil a legitimate role. The challenge is therefore to reassess the legitimate role of such shops. The proposition of shops and shopping centres has to change, as Primark has already successfully done. There will only be a future for shops if they can be relevant to customers once more.

The End of Development Aid?

Alibaba is a new concept that makes optimum use of the possibilities offered by technology. This applies to both the Internet and other facilities: communication, analyses, logistics and payments. A direct link between demand and producers is regarded as a new development of the Internet. 'Alibaba is reinventing the Internet' distressed American suppliers cry out. Alibaba is discovering anew the possibilities of the Internet. Changes in the sales function, the supply chain and, for example, the payment function are based on the customer's wishes and the possibilities offered by technology. Two aspects are of particular interest. First of all, the payments of the consumers do not go directly to the suppliers. The problem with direct payment is the risk of fraud. If the goods do not arrive or do not meet the customer's expectations, it is normally up to the customer to try to get his money back. In the case of Alibaba, the money is held until the customers approve payment. Only then is the money transferred to the manufacturer/supplier. If the customer has not received the goods, it is up to the supplier to prove otherwise. A track&trace system is a convenient feature for a customer, but is now a necessity for suppliers in order to provide proof that a delivery has been received.

A second important aspect is employment. Now that there is a direct connection between demand and supply, it is also possible for small manufacturers in remote places to be connected. Until recently youths in small Chinese villages left their homes for the big city in search of work. Now young people no longer need to leave their homes and villages. They can continue living in their own village whilst the small local plants and factories sell through Alibaba. This is the ultimate example of opening up deprived regions.

Development aid is not sufficient. Trade makes the difference. 'Better trade than aid' has long been an important motto, but has now become reality. So is it right that import duties have to be paid for the sales of these small plants and factories to wealthy countries with wealthy inhabitants? Is it not so that savings can now be made on development aid by buying from these poor people? Isn't this better for a stable development of these countries and for these deprived regions? Isn't this better for those people's self-esteem; work rather than aid?

So why are these people then punished with import duties from the country receiving the goods? Why is a policy enforced that discourages buying from these countries? The situation is even worse, as there is even a great disincentive to buy there due to the VAT charges and the imposition of import duties. Is the only reason that this is done because development aid comes from a different department than trade and industry?

What Will the Town Centres Look Like?

For decades local councils have enforced demotivating policies for shops in town centres. Everything was regulated, entrepreneurship was punished and customers were discouraged from coming to the city. The problem was that customers at the time had no other options. Parking costs increased and parking spaces were moved further away from shops. In the Netherlands the environmental lobby complained about the air quality in the city centres, so cars were banned; customers would just have to come by bike. The pavement was not to be used by retailers and shops were only allowed to stay open if the local council agreed; the same applied to bars and restaurants. Property tax increased each year and the public spaces were designed on the basis of necessity and safety, not on the basis of what was considered pleasant and desirable. This was fine as long as customers had no other choice. People without their own transportation had to shop in the city centre. But as time went by increasingly often people began to go to other city centres if those were more pleasant; yet this still represented a small percentage of the residents of any given town.

But all this has changed. First of all, due to the recession customers purchased less and more selectively. Thanks to the Internet it was suddenly possible to buy elsewhere and often at a lower price. And then the customer changed as well. Shopping became a choice, particularly for the non-daily purchases. Each year, the number of customers in shops dwindles; fewer customers who buy less. Furthermore, the customer is constantly connected to the Internet and knows precisely the price of the goods. If the shop is more expensive, the customer will simply buy online using his smartphone. The consequences can be seen in every town and city in the Netherlands: empty shop premises and retailers complaining about their reduced turnover and profit losses.

Shopping has become a choice, and the question is whether this choice is good for the town centre or shopping centre. Simply holding onto old structures will force customers to buy elsewhere. Obstacles that play a role are the accessibility of shops, the parking costs, the walking distance from the car to the shops and the shops' opening hours. In addition, there are all sorts of hedonistic aspects that play a role, such as experience, surroundings, inspiration, stimulation of the senses, services and convenience. Hopping onto the bike to go to the city centre is not a serious alternative. How can you take all your shopping home with you, and what if it rains?

Local councils stubbornly hold on to the current structures, as their budgets are based on them. Parking costs, municipal land taxes and property tax form an important part of a town council's budget and the largest component of the local taxes. Property owners and retailers pay the most when it comes to these local taxes. However, due to all these empty shop premises, local councils actually lose a great deal of money as a result of the reduced numbers of visitors to the city and a decline in parking revenues (also if the parking facilities are outsourced, agreements are often made regarding the parking policy and the minimum revenue). The result is a budgetary deficit.

In order to keep town centres attractive the local councils and property owners must develop a vision for their town centre. What will the town centre of the future be like? Ideally, a place that people like to visit and is easily accessible. Bars and restaurants, small shops and cultural activities will form part of the town centre, exactly like it was before the times of prosperity (the 1970s and earlier). Town centres have to go back to their roots, to find their own identity and character. There are examples that show this is in fact possible and that it improves the quality of life in a town.

Every town has to look at its DNA once again. What makes this town special and how can the residents be enticed to spend their money there? How can purchase flows be redirected towards the centre? The town centres of the future will become smaller and more compact, grouped around an epicentre, either the church, harbour or town square with surrounding bars and restaurants. Town centres will become places where it is pleasant to spend one's time. The number of single households will increase as they choose the vibrance of the town, and older residents will be attracted by the town's culture and restaurants. Town centres will no longer be the domain of large chain stores, which for decades determined the look of the cities' high streets, ultimately creating an undesired uniformity throughout the country. Town centres will become enjoyable and hedonistic, pleasant places in which to live and work (freelancers) and shops will raise the character of the town.

This is only possible if everyone is willing to work together on this and set their own self-interest aside. Local councils will have to facilitate the developments rather than direct them and take the behaviour and wishes of the residents as the guiding principle. The role of the town centres will change, the number of shops will decrease while bars and restaurants will become increasingly more important. There will be a new balance between living, shopping and working. A balance that is attractive for the residents. A town with a buzz is a town that's alive. Empty streets are the sign of a dead town.

The Future

The year 2015 marks the end of an era; the end of the supply economy and the further development of the demand economy. Customers demand a different type of shop, different shopping locations and a different type of product range. The Internet is developing into a new sort of platform that forms an integral part of our lives: for communication, for shopping and for supporting services such as payments. Technology will make dreams come true, and will make it possible to facilitate the fickle consumer of the future. Man as an individual will lie at the heart of these changes. People will make their choices and determine where they want to live, work and spend their leisure time. Emotions will once more play a leading role. We are human after all. Structures, processes and systems will be redefined not on the basis of yesterday's choices but on today's possibilities and wishes. Life will be different as a result, but certainly no less pleasant.

It is only a matter of wanting to change and adapt for everyone who wants to be part of this future that has begun today.

Bibliography

Al-Majali, F., and Prigmore, M. (2010). Consumers channel choice behavior in multi-channel environments: What are the influences on consumers to choose the online distribution channels over other alternative offline channels. In *Future Technologies in Computing and Engineering: Proceedings of Computing and Engineering Annual Researchers' Conference 2010*. University of Huddersfield, Huddersfield, UK.

Anderson, C. (2006). *The Long Tail*. London: Random House Business Books.

Arnold, M.J., and Reynolds, K.E. (2003). Hedonic shopping motivations. *Journal of Retailing*, 79(2), pp. 77–95.

Bloomberg.com. Alibaba Group company profile. Available at: http://www.bloomberg.com/profiles/companies/BABA:US-alibaba-group-holding-ltd [accessed 19 March 2015].

Brockman, J. and Hillis, W.D. (2011). *Is the Internet Changing the Way You Think? The Net's Impact on Our Minds and Future*. New York, NY: Harper Perennial.

Brynjolfsson, E., Hu, Y.J., and Rahman, M.S. (2013). Competing in the age of omnichannel retailing. *MIT Sloan Management Review*, 54(4).

Brynjolfsson, E., and McAfee, A. (2014). *The Second Machine Age*. New York, NY: W.W. Norton & Company Ltd.

Cap Gemini (2014). Digital Shopper Relevancy Research Report 2014. Available at: http://www.capgemini.com/resource-file-access/resource/pdf/dsr_2014_report_final.pdf [accessed 19 March 2015].

Castells, M. (2009). *Communication Power*. Oxford: Oxford University Press.

Christensen, C.M. (1997). *The Innovator's Dilemma: When New Technologies Cause Great Firms to Fail*. Boston, MA: Harvard Business School Press.

Collum, M. (2013). What factors affect customer's decisions when choosing to shop at out of town vs. in town retail centres? Case study: The Rock, Bury vs. The Trafford Centre. Dissertation, University of Central Lancashire. Available at: http://clok.uclan.ac.uk/9001/ [accessed 19 March 2015].

Daily Telegraph (2013). High street cheer on the cheap. 24 February. Available at: http://www.telegraph.co.uk/finance/newsbysector/retailand consumer/9895321/Primark-high-street-cheer-on-the-cheap.html [accessed 19 March 2015].

Daily Telegraph (2014a). Lidl sales to reach £4bn as pressure on supermarkets grows. 28 August. Available at: http://www.telegraph.co.uk/finance/ newsbysector/retailandconsumer/11059821/Lidl-sales-to-reach-4bn-as-pressure-on-supermarkets-grows.html [accessed 19 March 2015].

Daily Telegraph (2014b). Reality check for UK supermarkets. 30 August. Available at: http://www.telegraph.co.uk/finance/newsbysector/retailand consumer/11065646/Reality-check-for-UK-supermarkets.html [accessed 19 March 2015].

Daily Telegraph (2014c). Sainsbury's to cut stores and dividend. 8 November. Available at: http://www.telegraph.co.uk/finance/newsbysector/retailand consumer/11218851/Sainsburys-to-cut-stores-and-dividend.html [accessed 19 March 2015].

Daily Telegraph (2014d). Available at: http://www.telegraph.co.uk/technology/ news/11029448/High-street-shops-to-gets-high-tech-mannequins.html

Digitalbookworld.com (2014). Amazon booms in 2013 with $74.45 billion in revenue. 30 January. Available at: http://www.digitalbookworld.com/2014/ amazon-booms-in-2013-with-74-45-billion-in-revenue/

Downes, L., and Nunes, P. (2014). *Big Bang Disruption: Business Survival in the Age of Constant Innovation.* New York, NY: Portfolio Penguin.

Farber, D. (2014). Zuckerberg outlines Facebook's ambitious 10-year plan. 30 January Available at: http://www.cnet.com/news/zuckerberg-outlines-facebooks-ambitious-10-year-plan/ [accessed 19 March 2015].

Fast Company (2014). The $3.2 billion man: Can Google's newest star outsmart Apple? October, issue 189, p. 58.

Ferrazzi, K. (2014). Managing change, one day at a time. *Harvard Business Review*, July–August issue.

Fisher, M., and Raman, A. (2010). *The New Science of Retailing*. Boston, MA: Harvard Business Press.

Fishman, C. (2006). *The Walmart Effect*. Amsterdam: Business Contact.

Forbes.com (2013). How fashion retailer Burberry keeps customers coming back for more. 28 October. Available at: http://www.forbes.com/sites/sap/2013/10/28/how-fashion-retailer-burberry-keeps-customers-coming-back-for-more/ [accessed 19 March 2015].

Gladwell, M. (2002). *The Tipping Point: How Little Things Can Make a Big Difference*. New York, NY: Back Bay Books.

Green, R. (2014). *The Future of Shopping*. Adobe International.

Groenewegen, I. (2013). Enhancing the customer experience through the use of mobile shopping services in the retail store. MSc thesis, Rotterdam School of Management, Erasmus University.

Guardian, The (2014a). Grocers rush to open 'dark stores' as online food shopping expands. 6 January. Available at: http://www.theguardian.com/business/2014/jan/06/supermarkets-open-dark-stores-online-food-shopping-expands [accessed 19 March 2015].

Guardian, The (2014b). Morrisons reports its first month of sales growth since last autumn. 27 August. Available at: http://www.theguardian.com/business/2014/aug/27/uk-grocery-market-growth-price-inflation-supermarket [accessed 19 March 2015].

Hammond, R. (2011). *Smart Retail: Practical Winning Ideas and Strategies from the Most Successful Retailers in the World*. Harlow: Prentice Hall Business.

Hassan, B. (2010). Exploring gender differences in online shopping attitude. *Computers in Human Behavior*, 26(4), pp. 597–601 .

Human Behavior, 8 February 2010.

Independent, The (2013). Primark unlikely to continue with Asos online collaboration. 6 November. Available at: http://www.independent.co.uk/news/business/news/primark-unlikely-to-continue-with-asos-online-collaboration-8923652.html [accessed 19 March 2015].

iResearch.com (2014). With revenue of $7.5 billion in 2013, Alibaba restarts IPO. 24 March. Available at: http://www.iresearchchina.com/views/5541.html [accessed 19 March 2015].

Jantarajaturapath, P., and Ussahawanitchkit, P. (2009). E-commerce competencies and success of Thai e-commerce firms: A mediating of multi-channel retailing advantage. *Journal of Academy of Business and Economics, 9*(3), 1.

Kurzweil, R. (2005). *The Singularity is Near*. New York, NY: Penguin Books.

Laseter, T.M., and Rabinovich, E. (2012). *Internet Retail Operations: Integrating Theory and Practice For Managers*. Boca Raton, FL: CRC Press.

Lambin, J.-J. (2008). *Sub-Orientations in Market-Driven Management*. Louvain-la-Neuve: Presses universitaires de Louvain.

Lorange, P., and Rembiszewski, J. (2014). *From Great to Gone*. Farnham: Gower Publishing.

Ludin B., and Veira, S. (2013a). Gender differences and buying behaviour. Thesis, eMarketing, Rotterdam School of Management, Erasmus University.

Ludin B., and Veira, S. (2013b). Shopping choices: Online versus offline shopping, a psychological approach. Thesis, Rotterdam School of Management, Erasmus University.

MacKenzie, I., Meyer, C., and Noble, S. (2013). *How Retailers Can Keep Up with Consumers*. McKinsey & Company, October. Available at: http://www.mckinsey.com/insights/consumer_and_retail/how_retailers_can_keep_up_with_consumers [accessed 19 March 2015].

McQuivey, J. (2013). *Digital Disruption*. Las Vegas, NV: Amazon Publishing.

Molenaar, C.N.A. (2009). *Het nieuwe winkelen* [*The New Shop*]. Amsterdam: Pearson Education.

Molenaar, C.N.A. (2010). *Shopping 3.0: Shopping, the Internet or Both?* Farnham: Gower Publishing.

Molenaar, C.N.A. (2011). *Het Einde van Winkels?* [*The End of Shops?*] The Hague: Academic Services.

Molenaar, C.N.A. (2013). *Red de Winkel.* [*The Red Shop*]. The Hague: Academic Services.

Monsuwé, T.P., Dellaert, B.G.C., and de Ruyter, K. (2004). What drives consumers to shop online? A literature review? *International Journal of Service Industry Management, 15*(1), pp. 102–21

Niemeier, S., Zocchi, A., and Catena, M. (2013). *Reshaping Retail: Why Technology is Transforming the Industry and How to Win in the New Consumer Driven World.* Chichester: John Wiley & Sons.

O'Brien, H.L. (2014). The influence of hedonic and utilitarian motivations on user engagement: The case of online shopping experiences. *Interacting with Computers, 22*(5), pp. 344–52.

Pereira, L.C.P. (2014). Bluetooth, smart and iBeacon technology. Thesis, eMarketing, Rotterdam School of Management, Erasmus University.

Piskorski, M. (2014). What will Facebook look like in 10 years? Forbes. com, 4 March. Available at: http://www.forbes.com/sites/hbsworking knowledge/2014/03/04/what-will-facebook-look-like-in-2024/ [accessed 19 March 2015].

Readings Shop.org *Summit 2014*, Seattle, USA.

Retail Detail (2014). Coca-Cola geeft kortingen aan klanten in de buurt. 9 October. Available at: http://www.retaildetail.be/nl/in-beeld/item/19491-coca-cola-geeft-kortingen-aan-klanten-in-de-buurt [accessed 19 March 2015].

Retail Innovation (2012). US retailer Hointer uses robots to deliver your selections to the fitting room. Available at: http://retail-innovation.com/us-retailer-hointer-uses-robots-to-deliver-your-selections-to-the-fitting-room/ [accessed 10 March 2015].

Retailnews.nl (2014a). Delhaize tests the effects of beacons. 11 September. Available at: http://www.retailnews.nl/nieuws/hTZOnwBNRiufyj1jvQZldw -0/delhaize-test-inzet-van-beacons.html [accessed 10 March 2015].

Retailnews.nl (2014b). Media-Saturn sets his sights on online pure players. 24 October. Available at: http://www.retailnews.nl/nieuws/HqjI_ lrAEeSs4iIAClQRyw-6/media-saturn-zet-in-op-online-pure-players.html [accessed 10 March 2015].

Rifkin, J. (2014). The Zero Marginal Cost Society. New York, NY: Palgrave Macmillan.

Rossman, J. (2014). The Amazon Way. North Charleston, SC: Publishing Platform.

Saunders, R. (2000). De Amazon.com Business [Business the Amazon.com Way]. Rijswijk: Elmar.

Scarpi, D. (2012). Work and fun on the internet: The effects of utilitarianism and hedonism online. Journal of Interactive Marketing, 26(1), pp. 53–67.

Scarpi, D., Pizzi, G., and Visentin, M. (2014). Shopping for fun or shopping for need: Is it different online and offline? Journal of Retailing and Consumer Services, 21(3), pp. 258–67.

Schmidt, E., and Rosenberg, J. (2014). How Google Works. New York, NY: Grand Central Publishing.

Slywotzky, A.J., and Morrison, D.J. (1997). The Profit Zone: How Strategic Business Design Will Lead You to Tomorrow's Profits. New York, NY: Times Business.

Sorensen, H. (2009). Inside the Mind of the Shopper: The Science of Retailing. New York, NY: Pearson Education.

Stephens, D. (2013). The Retail Revival: Reimagining Business for the New Age of Consumerism. Toronto: John Wiley & Sons.

Stern, N. (2014). Retail Innovations 9: The Pace of Change Accelerates. Chicago, IL: Ebeltoft Group. Available at: http://www.ebeltoftgroup.com/retail-innovations3.html?aID=166166 [accessed 19 March 2015].

Stone, B. (2013a). The Everything Store: Jeff Bezos and the Age of Amazon. London: Transworld Publishers.

Stone, B. (2013b). *Mr. Amazon: de Onstuitbare Ambitie van Jeff Bezos* [*Mr Amazon: The Unstoppable Ambition of Jeff Bezos*]. Amsterdam: Business Contact.

Treacy, M., and Wiersema, F. (1995). *The Discipline of Market Leaders: Choose Your Customers, Narrow Your Focus, Dominate Your Market*. Reading, MA: Addison-Wesley.

Tuttle, B. (2013). The grocery store may be on its death-bed. *Time Business*, 8 October. Available at: http://business.time.com/2013/10/08/the-grocery-store-may-be-on-its-death-bed/ [accessed 19 March 2015].

van der Woud, A. (2012). *Koninkrijk Vol Sloppen. Achterbuurten en Vuil in de Negentiende Eeuw* [*A Kingdom of Slums. Back Streets and Dirt in the Nineteenth Century*]. Amsterdam: Bert Bakker.

van Keulen, C.H. (2014). Disruption analyses. Thesis, eMarketing, Rotterdam School of Management, Erasmus University.

van Lieshout, (2014). Customer journeys, online banking. Thesis, eMarketing, Rotterdam School of Management, Erasmus University.

van Wijnen, J.F. (2014). Disruptive innovation: Niets blijft het zelfde [Disruptive innovation: Nothing remains the same]. *Financieele Dagblad*, 1 February. Available at: http://fd.nl/Print/Bijlage/FD_Uitzicht/29664/disruptive-innovation-niets-blijft-hetzelfde [accessed 19 March 2015].

Vise, D.A., and Malseed, M. (2005). *The Google Story*. New York, NY: Bantam Dell.

Westerman, G., Bonnet, D., and McAfee, A. (2014). *Leading Digital: Turning Technology into Business Transformation*. Boston, MA: Harvard Business Review Press.

Yarrow, K. (2014). *Decoding the New Consumer Mind*. San Francisco, CA: Jossey-Bass.

Yarrow, K., and O'Donnell, J. (2009). *Gen BuY. How Tweens, Teens and Twenty-Somethings are Revolutionizing Retail*. San Francisco, CA: Jossey-Bass.

YouTube (2012). In-store Innovation at Tesco. Available at: https://www.youtube.com/watch?v=noa4SmYhjTA&index=4&list=FLFUeuO4yA8sAERFqGDd77qA [accessed 19 March 2015].

Index

Effective Client Management in Professional Services
How to Build Successful Client Relationships
Jack Berkovi
Hardback: 978-1-4094-3789-5
e-book PDF: 978-1-4094-3790-1
e-book ePUB: 978-1-4724-0798-6

What the New Breed of CMOs Know That You Don't
MaryLee Sachs
Hardback: 978-1-4094-5572-1
e-book PDF: 978-1-4094-5573-8
e-book ePUB: 978-1-4724-0404-6

The Irrational Consumer
Applying Behavioural Economics to Your Business Strategy
Enrico Trevisan
Hardback: 978-1-4724-1344-4
e-book PDF: 978-1-4724-1345-1
e-book ePUB: 978-1-4724-1376-5

Taking Technology to the Market
A Guide to the Critical Success Factors in Marketing Technology
Ian Linton
Hardback: 978-1-4094-3595-2
e-book PDF: 978-1-4094-3596-9
e-book ePUB: 978-1-4094-8330-4

Visit **www.gowerpublishing.com** and

- search the entire catalogue of Gower books in print
- order titles online at 10% discount
- take advantage of special offers
- sign up for our monthly e-mail update service
- download free sample chapters from all recent titles
- download or order our catalogue

DATE DUE

PRINTED IN U.S.A.